The Role of Religion in Public Policy

Other Books in the At Issue Series

America's Infrastructure
The Deep State
Ethical Pet Ownership
The Federal Budget and Government Spending
Gerrymandering and Voting Districts
Media Bias and the Role of the Press
Political Corruption
Politicians on Social Media
Presentism
The Role of Science in Public Policy
Troll Factories

At Issue

The Role of Religion in Public Policy

Eamon Doyle, Book Editor

LONGWOOD PUBLIC LIBRARY

Published in 2019 by Greenhaven Publishing, LLC
353 3rd Avenue, Suite 255, New York, NY 10010

Copyright © 2019 by Greenhaven Publishing, LLC

First Edition

All rights reserved. No part of this book may be reproduced in any form without permission in writing from the publisher, except by a reviewer.

Articles in Greenhaven Publishing anthologies are often edited for length to meet page requirements. In addition, original titles of these works are changed to clearly present the main thesis and to explicitly indicate the author's opinion. Every effort is made to ensure that Greenhaven Publishing accurately reflects the original intent of the authors. Every effort has been made to trace the owners of the copyrighted material.

Cover image: DanielW/Shutterstock.com

Library of Congress Cataloging-in-Publication Data

Names: Doyle, Eamon, 1988- editor.
Title: The role of religion in public policy / Eamon Doyle, book editor.
Description: First Edition. | New York : Greenhaven Publishing, 2019. | Series: At issue | Includes bibliographical references and index. | Audience: Grades 9-12.
Identifiers: LCCN 2018023307| ISBN 9781534503823 (library bound) | ISBN 9781534504516 (pbk.)
Subjects: LCSH: Church and state—United States. | Christianity and politics—United States. | United States—Politics and government. | Religion and state—United States. | Religion and politics—United States.
Classification: LCC BR516 .R65 2018 | DDC 322/.10973—dc23
LC record available at https://lccn.loc.gov/2018023307

Manufactured in the United States of America

Website: http://greenhavenpublishing.com

Contents

Introduction   7

1. Separation of Church and State   11
   D. James Kennedy
2. Faith, Democratic Politics, and the Secular Age   15
   Anthony Egan
3. Religion and Martin Luther King Jr.'s Civil Rights Advocacy   26
   Michael Curtotti
4. The Social Gospel Movement and the Religious Left   36
   Christopher H. Evans
5. Catholicism and the Tea Party   41
   John Gehring
6. Not All Scientists Are Atheists   47
   Amy McCaig
7. Topeka and the Westboro Baptist Church   51
   Southern Poverty Law Center
8. Supreme Court Rules in Favor of Westboro Baptist Church   65
   Nina Totenberg
9. The Social and Legal Dimensions of the US Evolution Debate   69
   David Masci
10. Catholicism and Politics in the Modern Era   82
    The Pontifical Academy of Social Sciences
11. American Attitudes on Religion in the Public Schools   100
    Pew Research Center
12. President Bush's Faith-Based Initiative   104
    Joseph Loconte
13. It's Time to Separate Church and State Marriages   107
    Bryan Cones

14. The Christian Right and the New Right **114**
    USHistory.org

Organizations to Contact **118**
Bibliography **122**
Index **126**

Introduction

The question of religion's role in public life is among civilization's oldest and most enduring controversies. Its history stretches back to the ancient Greek writers and probably much further. Many modern democracies (particularly in the West) have adopted formal legal boundaries to distinguish between religious and political authority and to assign specific rights and limitations to each sphere. In the United States, the First Amendment of the Constitution states that "Congress shall make no law respecting an establishment of religion, or prohibiting the free exercise thereof." This language, along with Thomas Jefferson's famous invocation of a "wall of separation between church and state" in an 1802 letter to the Danbury Baptist Association, has been at the center of America's now centuries-long debate on the proper boundaries of religion in society.

The preponderance of such boundaries in societies across the world is a phenomenon specific to modern history. In much of the premodern world there was little distinction between political and religious authority. Science (in the modern sense of the word) had not yet emerged as a major source of human knowledge, and liberal values like individual rights would have been considered esoteric and heretical. In this context, theocratic monarchy and other forms of religious oligarchy were the norm across the most complex and technologically advanced societies of the era.

It was the advent of Enlightenment values and modern secularism in the sixteenth and seventeenth centuries that eventually paved the way for a more dynamic political climate, first in Europe and eventually across the globe. The religious scholar Barry Bussey writes:

"The humanist strain of the Enlightenment stressed that reason provided the surest way for the affairs of man. Of greatest importance was that reason must triumph over religion and

> superstition. While religion was not disavowed entirely it was certainly put in a place where it could not control the power of the state to enforce its dogmas – its place was in the affairs of the individual, not of the state."[1]

Where political power had once been consolidated among a religious or political elite, it began to disperse into the commercial, military, religious, and technological spheres of society. The relative social equilibrium that emerged from competition between these spheres provided the basis for modern capitalism and democratic theory. New secular ideologies like Marxism, Liberalism, and Romantic Nationalism offered solidarity and a sense of purpose similar to what had only previously been available in a religious context, and politics across the West began to reorganize in terms of the right and the left. The writer Anthony Egan describes this process in the following passage:

> "Traditional religion was shaken at its foundations by the rise of nationalism, socialism and industrialisation. With the rise of communications to serve the latter in particular, small isolated communities that had been locked in a 'total' system including 'folk religion' were incorporated into larger economic and geographical units. They developed new identities outside the old system – whether as workers, Frenchmen, or through nationalist movements as Germans and Italians. These identities became, for most, primary."[2]

Some of the era's political philosophers (including Marx, Mill, and Nietzsche) imagined that religion, supplanted by these new ideologies, would fade from public life as the modern era continued to develop and evolve. But history has shown this prediction to be largely false, especially in the United States.

In spite of America's central role in the history of modern democracy and capitalism, the United States has a long tradition of religious revival and of religiously motivated political movements. The abolition movement, the temperance movement in the late nineteenth and early twentieth centuries, the civil rights movement in the sixties and seventies, the John Birch Society, and the modern

Evangelical movement (Reagan's "Moral Majority") have all justified and explained some of their political commitments in explicitly theological terms. Religious leaders and congregations are involved in voter turnout efforts, and religious organizations are involved in a wide variety of social welfare and advocacy activities. Several specific issues—including abortion, prayer and the teaching of evolution in public schools, same-sex marriage, and the death penalty—have emerged as flashpoints on the boundary between religion and politics in America. In some cases, such as the 2004 presidential election, electoral coalitions based around these issues have proven to be a decisive factor.[3]

In recent years, secular writers like Sam Harris, Steven Pinker, and Christopher Hitchens have offered an increasingly robust and fully articulated secular philosophy, incorporating elements of modern psychology and working to reframe social morality as a scientific project. Their ideas have attracted a wide audience, but have also raised the ire of religious conservatives and stoked fears of a liberal "war on Christianity," fears that figure prominently in the discourse of the so-called Alt-Right, which is emerging as a major political force in America. The writer and historian Benjamin E. Park writes:

"Americans, and especially American conservatives, are still devoted to proving the religious nature of their patriotic devotion. In a world of growing secularism, the United States is presented as a last refuge for explicit Christian devotion. The country's religious nationalism has even made possible one of the unlikeliest of alliances: the loyalty between evangelical ministers and Donald Trump. This quixotic marriage was only made possible due to a long tradition of patriotic piety and Christian partisanship, an uneven and dynamic trajectory that continues to produce new twists and turns."[4]

In other words, the issues, the orientation of conflict, and the partisan alignment will shift and evolve. But as long as religion remains a source of value and meaning to citizens, it will remain a factor on the public stage as well. *At Issue: The Role of Religion in Public Policy* takes a look at the various perspectives on the interaction between religion and politics. It allows for a better understanding of the historical basis of this uneasy union and offers a comprehensive look at opinions about the present and future of the issue.

Notes

1. Barry W. Bussey, "Liberal Democracy and Religion," Canadian Council of Christian Charities, July 23, 2013, https://www.cccc.org/news_blogs/barry/2013/07/23/liberal-democracy-and-religion/
2. "Does God Have a Vote? Faith, Democratic Politics and the Secular Age," by Anthony Egan, Helen Suzman Foundation, August 2011.
3. James Dao, "Same Sex Marriage Issue Key in Some G.O.P. Races," *The New York Times*, November 4, 2004, https://www.nytimes.com/2004/11/04/politics/campaign/samesex-marriage-issue-key-to-some-gop-races.html
4. Benjamin E. Park, "The Revolutionary Roots of America's Religious Nationalism," Religion & Politics, March 20, 2018, http://religionandpolitics.org/2018/03/20/the-revolutionary-roots-of-americas-religious-nationalism/

1

Separation of Church and State

D. James Kennedy

D. James Kennedy was a pastor, evangelist, Christian broadcaster, and author. He published a number of books on religious issues, including What If America Were a Christian Nation Again?

This viewpoint examines the origin of the phrase "separation of church and state" in Thomas Jefferson's 1802 letter to the Danbury Baptist Association, its connection to the religion clause in the First Amendment of the US Constitution, and how these concepts have evolved in the time since. The author argues that the phrase and the Establishment Clause are often misrepresented and misunderstood. Indeed, contrary to popular belief this wording does not appear in the Constitution at all.

"Separation of church and state" is a common metaphor that is well recognized. Equally well recognized is the metaphorical meaning of the church staying out of the state's business and the state staying out of the church's business. Because of the very common usage of the "separation of church and state phrase," most people incorrectly think the phrase is in the constitution. The phrase "wall of separation between the church and the state" was originally coined by Thomas Jefferson in a letter to the Danbury Baptists on January 1, 1802. His purpose in this letter was to assuage the fears of the Danbury, Connecticut Baptists, and so

---

"Separation Of Church And State," taken from *What if America Were a Christian Nation Again* by D. James Kennedy. Copyright © 2003 by D. James Kennedy. Used by permission of Thomas Nelson. www.thomasnelson.com.

he told them that this wall had been erected to protect them. The metaphor was used exclusively to keep the state out of the church's business, not to keep the church out of the state's business.

The constitution states, "Congress shall make no law respecting an establishment of religion, or prohibiting the free exercise thereof." Both the free exercise clause and the establishment clause place restrictions on the government concerning laws they pass or interfering with religion. No restrictions are placed on religions except perhaps that a religious denomination cannot become the state religion.

However, currently the implied common meaning and the use of the metaphor is strictly for the church staying out of the state's business. The opposite meaning essentially cannot be found in the media, the judiciary, or in public debate and is not any part of the agenda of the ACLU or the judiciary.

This, in conjunction with several other factors, makes the "separation of church and state" metaphor an icon for eliminating anything having to do with Christian theism, the religion of our heritage, in the public arena. One of these factors is the use of the metaphor in place of the actual words of the constitution in discourse and debate. This allows the true meaning of the words in the constitution to be effectively changed to the implied meaning of the metaphor and the effect of the "free exercise" clause to be obviated. Another factor facilitating the icon to censor all forms of Christian theism in the public arena is a complete misunderstanding of the "establishment" clause.

Separation of Church and State - The Establishment Clause in Context

In addition to the "Separation of Church and State" metaphor misrepresenting the words of the establishment clause, the true meaning of the establishment clause is also misrepresented. The "establishment" clause states, "Congress shall make no law respecting an establishment of religion. . ." Before these words can be put in context and the true meaning of the clause can be correctly identified, we need to examine the word "religion" and put it in America's historical context at the time the constitution was framed. In addition, we need to examine the previous European historical background of the founders of our country to identify what specifically motivated them to place the "establishment" clause in the constitution.

To accomplish this, we need to add more specificity to the word "religion" to clarify both the American and European historical backgrounds and put the word "religion" in proper context. We need to delineate between doctrinal and denominational religion. We also need to understand that the doctrinal religion being discussed is Christian Theism, which is defined by a belief in the Bible. We know what specific Christian denominational religions are.

Separation of Church and State - Constitution Framers Historical Context

The "Separation of Church and State" metaphor blurs the distinction between a doctrinal religion and a denominational religion. This places the doctrinal religion we have embraced in the same basket as an organized denominational religion with potential to merge with the state. The documentary evidence of the doctrinal Christian religion origin of this nation is voluminous. The Supreme Court thoroughly studied this issue, and in 1892 gave what is known as the Trinity Decision. In that decision the Supreme Court declared, "this is a Christian nation." John Quincy Adams said, "The highest glory of the American Revolution was, it connected in one indissoluble bond, the principles of civil government with the principles of Christianity." The founders were definitely Christian for the most part. At least 90 to 95 percentage of them were practicing, Trinitarian Christians. This and the additional supporting evidence below show conclusively that the concern that motivated the framers to include the establishment clause in the constitution was definitely not fear of the doctrinal religion of Christian Theism. It was understood that Christian Theism was the default state doctrinal religion. As opposed to being something to fear, it was something believed to be vital to the success of our government. Consequently, the framers feared a state denominational religion not a state doctrinal religion! Some additional evidences that indicate Christian Theism was the national doctrinal religion are listed below:

- Emblazoned over the Speaker of the House in the US Capitol are the words "In God We Trust."
- The Supreme Court building built in the 1930's has carvings of Moses and the Ten Commandments.
- God is mentioned in stone all over Washington D.C., on its monuments and buildings.
- As a nation, we have celebrated Christmas to commemorate the Savior's birth for centuries.
- Oaths in courtrooms have invoked God from the beginning.
- The founding fathers often quoted the Bible in their writings.
- Every president that has given an inaugural address has mentioned God in that speech.
- Prayers have been said at the swearing in of each president.
- Each president was sworn in on the Bible, saying the words, "So help me God."
- Our national anthem mentions God.
- The liberty bell has a Bible verse engraved on it.
- The original constitution of all 50 states mentions God.
- Chaplains have been in the public payroll from the very beginning.
- Our nations birth certificate, the Declaration of Independence, mentions God four times.
- The Bible was used as a textbook in the schools.

2

Faith, Democratic Politics, and the Secular Age

Anthony Egan

Dr. Anthony Egan, a Catholic priest and Jesuit, is a member of the Jesuit Institute of South Africa in Johannesburg. He is a research fellow at the Helen Suzman Foundation.

Anthony Egan provides a global historical overview of the relationship between religion and democracy, particularly looking at how that relationship has evolved in the era of modernity and secularization. In doing so, he responds to the so-called new atheists' strong critique of religion in public life. He argues that religion and secular democratic traditions are not necessarily at odds, though there have been historical clashes between the two.

[…]

Religious Belief and Democracy

Hard line new atheists seem to regard the intervention of any religious person in the public sphere with a mixture of fear and loathing. Any religious contribution is for them the beginning of a slippery slope from democracy back into the "dark ages"[1] of superstition and theocracy. They see the political mobilisation of fundamentalists as a dangerous threat to liberty, science and inquiry. Here one can only agree. The way that Christian fundamentalist groups have campaigned for their agenda in the United States is chilling, particularly when they use the institutions of democracy

"Does God have a Vote? Faith, Democratic Politics and the Secular Age," by Anthony Egan, Helen Suzman Foundation, August 2011. Reprinted by permission.

to impose bizarre Creationist views on school curricula. At their most extreme they have agitated for laws based on 'biblical' (read: literalist) interpretation and discrimination against non-Christians and non-believers. Similarly the rise of conservative movements of political Islam, in countries as varied as Iran and Saudi Arabia, have imposed antidemocratic social values on societies. Similar pressure groups are emerging from the other great religions of the world. At the most extreme, one sees the coupling of conservative religion and political violence in what might be called 'faith-based terrorist organisations'.

Are the new atheists right, then? Insofar as they select the most extreme religious groups and views, they are, to my mind, burning a straw man. Mainstream religion has evolved beyond extremism even if it remains uncomfortable with the secular state, with some sections of it perhaps hoping against hope for a return to the lost enchanted world under a sacred canopy. The challenge has been to generate an effective modus vivendi for religious organisations to engage positively and constructively with secular (post)modernity. For religious and secular moderates like ethicist Jeffrey Stout "[e]thical discourse in religiously plural modern democracies is secularized… only in the sense that it does not take for granted a set of agreed-upon assumptions about the nature and existence of God." You can't thus take for granted that "religious commitments have default authority in this context."[2]

However, before we take up Stout's challenge we need to first acknowledge that religions have had a profoundly ambivalent, often hostile, attitude to democracy and secularity. This is best illustrated by a potted account of a tradition, Christianity, and one important part of it, Roman Catholicism.

The Christian Church's Hostility to Democracy

Democracy should not be seen as foundational to Christianity, though churches today endorse it. There has been a long, turbulent history of mutual suspicion and hostility that has only really in the last two centuries eased into a generally healthy working relationship.

The *Judeo-Christian Scriptures* offer no direct endorsement of democracy. This is unsurprising given that democracy as such did not exist at the time: the political leitmotif was mostly one of kingship. God is King, Jesus is Lord. The early Christians organised along oligarchic lines prevalent in the Greco-Roman world without attempting to change the status quo. Christianity, though multi-class in composition, did not in the first centuries overthrow the dominant order, but Christianised it, and monarchical and later feudal politico-economic relationships predominated. This was brought to the world in the age of colonisation.

Religious minorities did indeed promote more egalitarian – what we might today call democratic – values and practices, drawing political analogies to biblical teachings about human dignity, equality of persons under God, and Christ's rejection of a class/ Coucaste system and incorporation of marginalised people (women, children, Samaritans, the ritually impure, the sick, etc).

And what happened to them? They were called heretics, persecuted and killed. From medieval penitential and millenarian movements, through the wars of the Reformation (where Luther sided with the German princes against the peasant movements of radical reformation, and where Calvin quickly imposed a theocracy of sorts in Geneva), through the 17th century religious wars and the English Civil War, democratic Christians were systematically exterminated.

Secularism and Democracy [3]

What started as an exposure and critique of corrupt church practices (i.e. the Reformation) moved into a critique of doctrine itself, culminating philosophically in intellectual deism and political liberalism that paved the way for the French Revolution, separation of church and state and ultimately modern secular democracy.[4] Liberalism and Romanticism, the two great intellectual movements of the 19th century, can thus be seen as the logical outcome not simply of Enlightenment atheism but as the logical extension of the Reformation into the politico-cultural spheres.

In "On Liberty" (1859) John Stuart Mill summed up the impact of such a movement on religion in politics:

> "Those who first broke the yoke of what called itself the Universal Church, were in general as little willing to permit difference of religious opinion as the Church itself. But when the heat of the conflict was over, without giving a complete victory to any party, and each church or sect was reduced to limit its hopes to retaining possession of the ground it already occupied; minorities, seeing they had no chance of becoming majorities, were under the necessity of pleading to those whom they could not convert, for permission to differ..."[5]

Mill's fundamental principle of liberty – self-protection of the individual from unnecessary and undue influence by society as a whole – expresses deep suspicion of any interventionist state, whether monarchical or democratic, theocratic or secular:

> "If all mankind minus one, were of one opinion, and only one person were of the contrary opinion, mankind would be no more justified in silencing that one person, than he, if he had the power, would be justified in silencing mankind."[6]

The next piece in the 19th century puzzle is the notion of Natural Supernaturalism,[7] both a literary cultural movement (Romanticism) and the culmination of the Reformation-Enlightenment movement away from medieval religio-political and cultural cosmology through deism towards modern atheism. Old religious practices and eschatology gave way to an emphasis on this-worldly salvation and humanist theologies that questioned the classical religious system. Much theology became, as John Kent noted, rooted in "the historical approach; the concomitant rejection of Verbal Inspiration theories; anti-dogmatism; the tendency to prefer existentially defined 'religions' to creeds, confessional statements and propositional theology in general".[8] Here too we see Charles Taylor's theory of disenchantment and the rise of expressive individualism in the very discourse of Christian religion itself.

Traditional religion was shaken at its foundations by the rise of nationalism, socialism and industrialisation. With the rise of communications to serve the latter in particular, small isolated communities that had been locked in a 'total' system including 'folk religion' (the remnants of Taylor's 'enchanted world') were incorporated into larger economic and geographical units. They developed new identities outside the old system – whether as workers, Frenchmen, or through nationalist movements as Germans and Italians. These identities became, for most, primary: in the face of scientific rationalism and modernity, the old religious verities also crumbled.

As secular democratic ideas gained ground, the churches almost universally sided with the *ancien regime*. Some were more explicit than others. A succession of 19th century popes denounced liberalism and democracy as heretical. Pius IX, after the 1848 revolutions in Europe, intransigently resisted the Italian unification and the assimilation of the Papal States became unstoppable. This found expression in the 1864 *Syllabus of Errors*, with its stinging attack on the 'evils' of the 19th century – pantheism, naturalism, absolute or moderate rationalism, indifferentism, latitudinarianism, socialism, communism, secret societies, bible societies, clerico-liberal societies, restrictions on the Church's (or pontiff's) political powers or civil and educational rights, in short the very notion that the "Roman pontiff can and ought to reconcile and harmonize himself with progress, with liberalism, and with modern civilization."[9]

The pope's political power ultimately collapsed with the final annexation of Rome in 1871. For decades after the unification of Italy popes denounced the constitutional monarchy, threatening any Catholic who voted (or joined a party) with excommunication. [10] Gradually this changed. Faced with radical anti-clericalism and socialism, the Catholic Church rather reluctantly endorsed democracy more as a lesser evil than a good that could be drawn out analogically from scripture, tradition and reason.

Why were the churches uneasy with democracy? I think the reason lay in their (quite justifiable) sense that democratic politics would undermine religious authority. In an era of *cuius regius eius religio* (religion of the ruler dictates religion of the ruled) and notions of the divine right of kings, the social order mirrored the religious order of popes, bishops, priests and 'the rest', with similar notions occurring in protestant traditions, e.g. the monarch as head of the Church of England or Scandinavian Lutheran traditions, the dominance of church leaders in Calvinist states. Not to be of the faith of the ruler was unpatriotic; to call for religious tolerance was to drive a wedge between spiritual and temporal authority, leading to a secular state.

The popes were right in their judgment, but their actions proved futile and alienated them from modern society. The wedge between temporal and spiritual was firmly driven into popular consciousness.

In 1893 Pope Leo XIII introduced what became known as Catholic Social Thought in his encyclical *Rerum Novarum*, partly an attempt by the church to engage with the wider world. This and subsequent encyclicals were characterised by an appeal to secular philosophical reasoning to provide a common language for discussion. By calling the Second Vatican Council (1962-65) Pope John XXIII further tried to bring the church into dialogue with secularity, trying to build up common ground with other churches and societies. This *aggiornamento* can be seen as an attempt to bring the church into the new secular reality – dialogue with modernity and the values of democracy and human rights within society. *Aggiornamento* was the Catholic Church's attempt to embrace and engage with the *fait accompli* of the secular age.

It was not, however, welcomed by everyone. Many objected that any accommodation with modernity was compromising the faith. This created insecurity and crises of identity. While some churches effectively turned their backs on modernity and retreated from the early 20th century into biblical fundamentalism, the Catholic Church from 1965 onwards became a battle ground between modernisers and restorationists. Restorationism started in about 1968. While promoting a political progressivism that supported political democratisation and economic justice on every continent, the church leadership, no doubt with an eye on Vatican I, centralised ecclesial authority, tightened theological and clerical discipline and remained uncompromising on personal moral issues. This rejection of democracy, as Margaret Farley has noted,

> *"awakens old fears (whether fairly or not) of nondemocratic organizations overly influencing a democratic society. It raises suspicions (whether legitimately or not) of hidden agendas, manipulation by external powers, and loyalties not appropriate for participation in a democratic process. Once again, the credibility of the church's political agenda, and its calls for justice, are compromised."[11]*

Authoritarian attitudes in the Church, and claims to 'special authority' based on anthropologies and certain forms of reasoning not shared by everyone – though they may have no relation to its socio-political stance in many areas – have an impact on how the church is perceived by the state, by non-Catholics and by many Catholics too.

Redefining Religion's Role in Democracy

How then does religion fit into democracy today? Philosopher Robert Audi[12] proposes that in a secular liberal democracy we need to adhere to three guiding principles for church-state relations:

- *Libertarian Principle.* The state must permit any religion to function, within the limits of civil and criminal law [13] (tolerance). While the state does not necessarily approve of a religion it recognises its right to exist.
- *Equalitarian Principle.* The state gives no preference to one religion over another (impartiality). In short there is no established church.
- *Neutrality Principle.* The state should neither favour nor disfavour religion as such (no favouritism).[14]

Such principles should apply in both directions, he suggests: state to church and church to state. This does not apply in a dictatorship where religions may feel compelled to exercise their role in opposing tyranny, but in a functioning democracy where secular structures exist to exercise influence on society. Going through these structures is the process whereby society, including the religions, can exercise influence on governance.

Audi does not naively presume that there is a disconnection between the political and the moral. Morality and politics are inevitably connected; what he is against is a particular morality imposed on everyone, particularly where such a morality is rooted in a theological set of presuppositions which may disadvantage the exercise of the two foundational ideas of liberal democracy namely personal liberty and basic political equality.

Unlike some philosophers, Audi does not rule out religious arguments but merely insists that they should not be the foundational or sole foundations for a church's political engagement, since they do not necessarily hold the same value for believers as for unbelievers (or indeed, one might add, be shared by believers within a particular church or religious tradition). A religious argument advanced in a democracy has to be conscious of the degree to which its content is founded on a particular religious belief, the way it uses empirical and other evidence to justify itself, its motivation, and the historical pedigree of its argument.[15] Its argument should not simply be based on some 'conversation-stopper' rooted in unverifiable 'divine revelation', claims based on scriptures or doctrines not everyone shares or on claims to the authority of religious leaders. Audi is deeply concerned about many of the phenomena and ways in which religions conduct themselves in trying to pursue their religio-political agenda, including:

- infallible expressions of authority
- condemnatory tendencies
- threats of religious domination
- tendencies towards cults and fundamentalisms

- attitudes of self-importance
- obsessions with outsiders, and
- other features that often prefigure institutional intolerance. [16]

Aggressive, authoritarian expression of a position may result, rather than moderation, prudence and openness to dialogue. Fallibility, recognition of limitations and openness to change are values Audi and other democrats prize. Indeed, they are a *sine qua non* of democracy.

To those who object that secular reasoning as pursued in democracy is fallible because it is human, Audi responds that religious reasoning is equally fallible.[17] Given that one cannot prove that such reasoning, whether from scriptures or authority, is truly divine (unless one accepts it as such) – and only divine for those who share in the particular religion – religious reasoning cannot legitimately be privileged, let alone when religious reasonings are themselves contradictory between and within religions.

There is also the danger within religious reasoning that it bases its secular reasoning on unverifiable religious presuppositions couched in secular language. At best this may simply be naivety on the part of religious activists who cannot see that what they're saying is fundamentally based on faith, not scientific evidence; at worst it may be intellectual dishonesty and manipulation.

Should religion say anything, then? Unlike rabid secularists, Audi thinks they should. "Reason without intuition", he argues, "is at best too formal to guide everyday life" but "faith requires reason to interpret its objects and human life in general; and the traditions most worthy of our attention surely reflect reason in major ways or at least depend on it for their interpretation."[18] Religious intuitions, although not based on cold empirical facts, may offer insights that need to be addressed, may open areas of debate that may be overlooked. But, Audi insists, when dealing with questions of policy, religions should advance arguments that are basically rational and secular in content and form.

A Conclusion (of Sorts)

Despite the revival of religion in many parts of the world, a revival that some like the sociologist Peter Berger see as a refutation of the secularisation thesis he and others previously espoused, such a revival in democratic societies has not had the effect of turning the clock back. Secularisation, in the sense of a decline in religious belief and practice, may not be as universal as previously thought. But this, Taylor has reminded us, is not the essence of secularisation.

Religious revival and the political power of religion in some places may well be a sign of the *failure* of democratic states in some places – where the state infrastructure is weak, where confidence in democratic governance is weak, religions may even serve as an alternative government. But this is no guarantee that a change of fortunes – a renewal of democracy, effective governance, economic and social recovery – will not sweep away the 'gains' made by religion. Apart from the moral dubiousness of religions 'cashing in' on human misfortune, this seems merely to be delaying the inevitable. It also disempowers religions by giving them an overinflated sense of self-importance, promotes leadership by power-mongers, and 'de-skills' religions from learning how to cope with living in a democratic environment.

Personally, as one who is both a religious person and a strong supporter of the secular democratic tradition, I am convinced that the kind of approach outlined by Robert Audi is something religious institutions and believing citizens should welcome. In South Africa one sees how Audi's model actually works – in the shape of the Catholic Parliamentary Liaison Office in Cape Town, a body formed by the Southern African Catholic Bishops' Conference to engage with Parliament in policy formulation and debate. Similar groups have been established by the South African Council of Churches and by the Muslim community. Neither anointing the secular nor condemning it, they debate with policy makers in secular terms, albeit informed by their faith traditions.

In this, they are robust exemplars of how religions engage with democracy in the secular age.

Notes

[1] A myth, argues Stark (2003), quite convincingly. Rodney Stark, 2003. *For the Glory of God: How Monotheism Led to Reformations, Science, Witch-Hunts, and the End of Slavery* (Princeton NJ: Princeton University Press).

[2] Jeffrey Stout, 2004. *Democracy and Tradition* (Princeton, NJ: Princeton University Press), 99.

[3] Parts of this section are drawn on an article I published some years back: Anthony Egan, 2000. "The Crisis of modernity and the 'invention' of Vatican I", *The Month*, December, 469-473.

[4] S. J. Barnett, 1999. *Idol Temples and Crafty Priests: The Origins of Enlightenment Anticlericalism* (New York: St Martin's Press).

[5] John Stuart Mill, 1961. *Essential Works of John Stuart Mill* (New York: Bantam Books), 261

[6] Ibid., 269.

[7] Cf. M. H. Abrams, 1971. *Natural Supernaturalism: Tradition and Revolution in Romantic Writing* (New York: W. W. Norton).

[8] John H. S. Kent, 1982. *The End of the Line: The Development of Christian Theology in the Last Two Centuries* (Philadelphia: Fortress Press), 23-4.

[9] Syllabus of Errors (1864).

[10] Cf. David I. Kertzner, 2004. *Prisoner of the Vatican* (Boston: Houghton Mifflin).

[11] Margaret A. Farley, 2001. "The Church in the Public Forum: Scandal or Prophetic Witness?", in: Charles E Curran & Leslie Griffin (eds.), *The Catholic Church, Morality and Politics* (New York: Paulist Press), 215.

[12] Robert Audi, 2000. *Religious Commitment and Secular Reason* (Cambridge: Cambridge University Press).

[13] How the state may limit religious freedom where it violates civil-criminal law is suggested by McLean (1997). Graeme R. McLean, 1997 "Freedom of Religion and State Neutrality: A Philosophical Problem." *South African Law Journal* 174.

[14] Audi (2000), 32-33.

[15] Ibid., 69-75.

[16] Ibid., 100-103.

[17] Ibid., 138.

[18] Ibid., 215.

3

Religion and Martin Luther King Jr.'s Civil Rights Advocacy

Michael Curtotti

Michael Curtotti is a writer, religious scholar, and the founder of the website Beyond Foreignness.

In this viewpoint, Michael Curtotti examines how Dr. Martin Luther King Jr.'s experience as a Baptist minister helped to shape the ideas and advocacy that would turn him into a civil rights leader. Through examining the relationship between the American civil rights movement and Christianity, Curtotti makes the argument that religion has played a major role in how human rights are defined and defended.

Martin Luther King Jr. was born in Atlanta Georgia, the second son of Martin Luther King Sr. and Alberta Williams King.

Martin Luther King Jr. was by vocation a Baptist minister. He was in the fourth generation of his family to take up this vocation. It is impossible to fully appreciate Martin Luther King's work without understanding the role that Christian thought and inspiration played in his advocacy of human rights.

Martin Luther King's letter from a Birmingham prison to fellow Christian clergymen gives insight to the role his religious commitment played in generating and sustaining his commitment to work for justice. Further, the people from whom he came, the

"Martin Luther King Jr. – What Role Did Christianity Play in his Civil Rights Advocacy?" by Michael Curtotti, Beyond Foreignness, September 19, 2014. Reprinted by permission.

African Americans who struggled against centuries of slavery and racism, drew from deep spiritual and human reservoirs in the long and bitter journey from slavery, through oppression and segregation, before the civil rights reforms were won.

In setting out why he was in Birmingham he explicitly drew on a 'prophetic role'.

> *"I am in Birmingham because injustice is here. Just as the prophets of the eight century B.C. left their villages and carried their "thus saith the Lord" far beyond the boundaries of their home towns … so I am compelled to carry the gospel of freedom beyond my home town."*

In explaining the nonviolent methods he practised, criticism of which he was responding to, he wrote: "We have waited more than 340 years for our constitutional and God-given rights."

He drew on biblical precedents for civil disobedience to the law, "*on the ground that a higher moral law was at stake.*"Al Human rights, as he conceived them, do not depend on the decision of any human agency. As a consequence, they can never be overridden by any human decision. It is a perspective which in the final analysis places human rights beyond the reach of any tyrant, no matter how powerful, and beyond the reach of any rationalisation offered by the powerful that claims a justification for the oppression of human beings.

In thinking about Martin Luther King's Christianity, we would again miss something significant to his human rights advocacy if we didn't consider how his spiritual practice was engaged in that work. The role that prayer played in Martin Luther King's work, is captured in a recollection from his wife Coretta King.

> *Prayer was a wellspring of strength and inspiration during the Civil Rights Movement. Throughout the movement, we prayed for greater human understanding. We prayed for the safety of our compatriots in the freedom struggle. We prayed for victory in our nonviolent protests, for brotherhood and sisterhood among people of all races, for reconciliation and the fulfillment of the Beloved Community.*

> *For my husband, Martin Luther King, Jr. prayer was a daily source of courage and strength that gave him the ability to carry on in even the darkest hours of our struggle.*
>
> *I remember one very difficult day when he came home bone-weary from the stress that came with his leadership of the Montgomery Bus Boycott. In the middle of that night, he was awakened by a threatening and abusive phone call, one of many we received throughout the movement. On this particular occasion, however, Martin had had enough.*
>
> *After the call, he got up from bed and made himself some coffee. He began to worry about his family, and all of the burdens that came with our movement weighed heavily on his soul. With his head in his hands, Martin bowed over the kitchen table and prayed aloud to God: "Lord, I am taking a stand for what I believe is right. The people are looking to me for leadership, and if I stand before them without strength and courage, they will falter. I am at the end of my powers. I have nothing left. I have nothing left. I have come to the point where I can't face it alone."*
>
> *Later he told me, "At that moment, I experienced the presence of the Divine as I had never experienced Him before. It seemed as though I could hear a voice saying: 'Stand up for righteousness; stand up for truth; and God will be at our side forever.'" When Martin stood up from the table, he was imbued with a new sense of confidence, and he was ready to face anything. (Coretta King – Standing in the Need of Prayer)*

If one happens not to share Martin Luther King's faith, what meaning can be drawn from what is described here? Within the act of prayer, part of what is described is Martin Luther King's search for and discovery of knowledge in a time of deep uncertainty.

Another article considers the semi-autobiographical work, *The Strange Alchemy of Life and Law* by, Justice Albie Sachs. From South Africa, much of Justice Sach's life has also been devoted to human rights through the struggle against apartheid, as well as to law. Justice Sachs describes himself as Jewish but non-religious: "not practising in any way". Yet he states in his book: "I did in fact have a strong set of beliefs, my own world view, in many ways a deeply spiritual one with overwhelming ethical implications." Speaking of solving problems in the law, he speaks about moments of inspiration as being the most creative and productive: "only when I had been close to being in what my Buddhist friends would call a transcendental meditational state, would these formulations emerge, as if from nowhere … it so happened that the first three times I was cited in foreign jurisdictions, the formulations had all come to me at moments when my brain had been least engaged in hard legal reasoning." Looked at in ways that transcend mere words, there is much that is common in the human experience. The inner resources that Martin Luther King drew upon do not depend on how we choose to describe ourselves nor on the particular model of reality we may hold. They likely do depend on some form of engagement with our inner "spiritual" life; however we might describe it.

Most poignantly, the deep spirituality of Martin Luther King's journey, is captured in the final words of the speech he delivered the evening before his murder. There were fears that evening. Threats had been made. He spoke of how happy he was to live in the time of the civil rights movement, having survived an earlier assassination attempt, and having seen the victories that had been won. How happy he was to have lived long enough to undertake the work he felt he had to do, and had now completed. In his last words he was a Moses to his people.

> *"Well, I don't know what will happen to me now. We've got some difficult days ahead. But it doesn't matter what happens to me now. Because I've been to the mountaintop. And I don't mind. Like anybody, I would like to live a long life. Longevity has its place. But I'm not concerned about that now. I just want to do God's will. And He's allowed me to go up to the mountain. And I've looked over. And I've seen the promised land. I may not get there with you. But I want you to know tonight that we, as a people will get to the promised land. And I'm happy tonight. I'm not worried about anything. I'm not fearing any man. Mine eyes have seen the glory of the coming of the Lord."*

The spiritual roots of human rights on which he drew, are also seen in his speech titled "the American Dream", delivered in 1964, where he spoke on the concept of rights, as found in the US Declaration of Independence. He says of its well known opening phrases affirming the core values of human rights that, "This is a dream." He means it is a dream that neither existed at the time the Declaration was originally written, nor did it exist in his own day. He identifies as distinctive of this dream that: "It says that each individual has certain basic rights that are neither derived from nor conferred by the state. They are gifts from the hands of the Almighty God."

In his speech in 1964 accepting the Nobel Peace Prize his words speak of the power of "faith". In this case his words are not so much addressing "religious" faith, as addressing a "faith" that sustains the struggle against oppression, even in the direst circumstances.

"I refuse to accept the view that mankind is so tragically bound to the starless midnight of racism and war that the bright daybreak of peace and brotherhood can never become a reality. …

"I still believe that mankind will bow before the altars of God and be crowned triumphant over war and bloodshed … I still believe that we shall overcome.

"This faith can give us courage to face the uncertainties of the future. It will give our tired feet new strength as we continue our forward stride toward the city of freedom. When our days become dreary with low-hovering clouds and our nights become darker than a thousand midnights, we will known that we are living in the creative turmoil of a genuine civilization struggling to be born."

These are the words of a man and a people whose faith have sustained them through centuries of oppression.

In international fora, and in the 21st century, human rights work is generally carried on without reference to any 'higher authority'.

In part, this is a consequence of the need for universality – the necessity of adopting and speaking a language and concepts that are accessible for all human beings irrespective of historical background and irrespective of belief. Of using language that does not exclude the dreams of any human being for justice. Thus when, in 1948, the Universal Declaration of Human Rights re-expressed "the dream", it did not mention "God". Not because faith was not important to a number of those involved in the creation of the Declaration, but because those involved felt this new language should be a wider dream inclusive of all human beings irrespective of "belief".

Their insight was of course right.

However a heavy price is paid if, from a justifiable concern for universality, we disconnect human rights from its genuine *human* history.

One price, is the unmooring of human rights from the lives of the human beings who gave us human rights. Many, as a matter of historical fact, were motivated by their religious beliefs. Many were not. But human rights cannot be understood if the actual stories of the human beings involved are not told and re-told. Each story gives us new insight. Where that story includes faith, it requires neither minimisation nor excuse. Rather the insights that they offer need to be gathered and contributed back into the flow of today's and tomorrow's human rights work. Without these human stories, the roots of human rights are stripped of their humanity. It was real human beings, with deep and complex motivations, who gave us human rights. By walking alongside them through their stories as they struggle to realise human rights, we learn what universality of human rights means far more deeply than from any philosophical argument.

Further if we do not tell the real history, other narratives are substituted that impoverish human rights history. Paul Gilroy in his oration *Race and the Right to be Human* has captured this well.

> We meet this evening close to the 61st anniversary of the Universal Declaration of Human Rights. As it became popular and influential, the political idea of human rights acquired a particular historical trajectory. The official genealogy it was given is extremely narrow. The story of its progressive development is usually told ritualistically as a kind of ethno-history. In that form,

> it contributes to a larger account of the moral and legal ascent of Europe and its civilizational offshoots.
>
> The bloody histories of colonization and conquest are rarely allowed to disrupt that linear, triumphalist tale of cosmopolitan progress. Struggles against racial or ethnic hierarchy are not viewed as an important source or inspiration for human rights movements and ideologies. Advocacy on behalf of indigenous and subjugated peoples does not, for example, merit more than token discussion as a factor in shaping how the idea of universal human rights developed and what it could accomplish.

Needless to say, this substitute history is deeply inaccurate. In words that Martin Luther King might use, the "ought" of human rights and human aspiration is displaced and substituted by the "is" of the status quo. This status quo was, in Martin Luther King's time, and remains in many ways in our own, profoundly unjust. To let an unjust present appropriate and clothe itself in human rights, places a high and unjustified barrier in the way further human rights progress. It disempowers those who like Martin Luther King, seek a better future than today.

Thirdly there is a specific methodology which human rights forebears like Martin Luther King employed with great effect in the cause of human rights. This methodology is lost when human rights are unmoored from its history. Gilroy refers to this aspect as "sentimentality". The language of human rights, at its most effective, speaks both to the human mind and to the human heart, as Martin Luther King did. Others well before him also use language of both heart and mind, as Paul Gilroy also notes:

> [Angelina] Grimké elaborated upon this inspired refusal of the reduction of people to things in a memorable (1838) letter to her friend Catherine Beecher (the older sister of Harriet Beecher Stowe). ….:
> "The investigation of the rights of the slave has led me to better understanding of our own. I have found the Anti- slavery cause to be the high school of morals in our land—the school in which human rights are more fully investigated and better understood and taught, than in any other. Here a great fundamental

principle is uplifted and illuminated, and from this central light rays innumerable stream all around. Human beings have rights, because they are moral beings: the rights of all men grown out of their moral nature, they have essentially the same rights."

Again the exclusion of these aspects of human rights create a vacuum which is filled with an imagined reality lacking genuineness and disconnected from the human beings who struggled for human rights.

That imagined reality sometimes has the character of a dry and soulless legalism that reduces the great principles and values of human rights to mere rules to be forensically applied to determine a legal outcome. They implicitly substitute treaty rules and legal regulation for true humanity and a true spirit of "brotherhood". As we saw, above, Martin Luther King, was well aware that human rights do not come from documents: "*they are neither conferred by nor derive from the state."*

Gandhi perhaps captured this well when responding to a letter from UNESCO asking for input towards the drafting of the Universal Declaration of Human Rights. The substance of his reply is brief:

"I'm afraid I can't give you anything approaching your minimum. That I have no time for the effort is true enough. But what is truer is that I am a poor reader of literature past or present much as I should like to read some of its gems. Living a stormy life since my early youth, I had no leisure to do the necessary reading.

I learnt from my illiterate but wise mother that all rights to be deserved and preserved come from duty well done. Thus the very right to live accrues to us only when we do the duty of citizenship of the world. From this one fundamental statement, perhaps it is easy enough to define the duties of Man and Woman and correlate every right to some corresponding duty to be first performed. Every other right can be shown to be an usurpation hardly worth fighting for."

Indirectly, Gandhi expresses a source of human rights which is far deeper than any documentary, or even philosophical source.

He communicates a life of struggle that billions have faced over history, and continue to face today: a life in which there is no leisure to read. It is from these human beings that the universal cry for justice has echoed through history. He also expresses human rights in terms that anyone in the human rights movement will understand. Human rights are not achieved without taking up our duty to contributing to their realisation.

Eleanor Roosevelt put it this way on the tenth anniversary of the Universal Declaration of Human Rights.

> *"Where, after all, do universal human rights begin? In small places, close to home – so close and so small that they cannot be seen on any maps of the world. Yet they are the world of the individual person; the neighbourhood he lives in; the school or college he attends; the factory, farm or office where he works. Such are the places where every man, woman and child seeks equal justice, equal opportunity, equal dignity without discrimination. Unless these rights have meaning there, they have little meaning anywhere. Without concerned citizen action to uphold them close to home, we shall look in vain for progress in the larger world."*

There are numerous insights we can draw from the spiritual foundations of Martin Luther King's work, irrespective of our own beliefs. Not only does each of us have human rights, we owe them to no human institution. We possess human rights "inherently" in our humanity. The struggle for a more just world is a shared struggle and we have a right and obligation to stand for others human rights, just as much as our own. Human rights are as much a characteristic of the human heart as the human mind. As much as laws may assist in the realisation of human rights; they are an inadequate repository for them. Only the human heart is sufficiently expansive to contain them. The struggle for human rights requires faith in our ability as human beings to create a more just order. It requires us to draw on our inner 'spiritual' reserve. No matter how dark the immediate horizon may be; no matter how far the dawn; the day will come when the oppressions of today are no more.

There is something else. In a world that is in our own day so publicly secular and sometimes distrustful of the contribution that religion might make; something is surprising. We have largely forgotten how recently it was, that Christianity played a pivotal role in one of the key human rights struggles of history.

4

The Social Gospel Movement and the Religious Left

Christopher H. Evans

Christopher H. Evans is a professor of history at Boston University and author of Histories of American Christianity: An Introduction *and* Liberalism without Illusions: Renewing an American Christian Tradition *and editor of* The Social Gospel Today, *among other titles.*

Christopher H. Evans examines the social gospel movement in the late nineteenth century as an example of religion's influence on the politics of the Left in the United States. Evans argues that religion has had a long history of influencing social movements in the United States, citing key examples from the nation's history to support this assertion. While the religious Right has historically had a more public image in American politics, Evans argues that religion has also had a strong influence on the Left.

Throughout American history, religion has played a significant role in promoting social reform. From the abolitionist movement of the early 19th century to the civil rights movement of the 20th century, religious leaders have championed progressive political causes.

This legacy is evident today in the group called religious progressives, or the religious left.

"How the Social Gospel Movement Explains the Roots of Today's Religious Left," by Christopher H. Evans, The Conversation, July 18, 2017. https://theconversation.com/how-the-social-gospel-movement-explains-the-roots-of-todays-religious-left-78895. Licensed under CC BY-ND 4.0 International.

The social gospel movement of the late 19th and early 20th centuries, as I have explored in my research, has had a particularly significant impact on the development of the religious left.

What is the social gospel movement and why does it matter today?

What Was the Social Gospel?

The social gospel's origins are often traced to the rise of late 19th-century urban industrialization, immediately following the Civil War. Largely, but not exclusively, rooted in Protestant churches, the social gospel emphasized how Jesus' ethical teachings could remedy the problems caused by "Gilded Age" capitalism.

Movement leaders took Jesus' message "love thy neighbor" into pulpits, published books and lectured across the country. Other leaders, mostly women, ran settlement houses designed to alleviate the sufferings of immigrants living in cities like Boston, New York and Chicago. Their mission was to draw attention to the problems of poverty and inequality – especially in America's growing cities.

Charles Sheldon, a minister in the city of Topeka, Kansas, explained the idea behind the social gospel in his 1897 novel "In His Steps." To be a Christian, he argued, one needed to walk in Jesus's footsteps.

The book's slogan, "What would Jesus do?" became a central theme of the social gospel movement which also became tied to a belief in what Ohio minister Washington Gladden called "social salvation." This concept emphasized that religion's fundamental purpose was to create systemic changes in American political structures.

Consequently, social gospel leaders supported legislation for an eight-hour work day, the abolition of child labor and government regulation of business monopolies.

While the social gospel produced many important figures, its most influential leader was a Baptist minister, Walter Rauschenbusch.

The Legacy of Walter Rauschenbusch

Rauschenbusch began his career in the 1880s as minister of an immigrant church in the Hell's Kitchen section of New York. His 1907 book, "Christianity and the Social Crisis" asserted that religion's chief purpose was to create the highest quality of life for all citizens.

Rauschenbusch linked Christianity to emerging theories of democratic socialism which, he believed, would lead to equality and a just society.

Rauschenbusch's writings had a major impact on the development of the religious left in the 20th century. After World War I, several religious leaders expanded upon his ideas to address issues of economic justice, racism and militarism.

Among them was A.J. Muste, known as the "American Gandhi," who helped popularize the tactics of nonviolent direct action. His example inspired many mid-20th century activists, including Martin Luther King Jr.

The intellectual influences on King were extensive. However, it was Rauschenbusch who first made King aware of faith-based activism. As King wrote in 1958,

> *"It has been my conviction ever since reading Rauschenbusch that any religion which professes to be concerned about the souls of men and is not concerned about the social and economic conditions that scar the soul, is a spiritually moribund religion only waiting for the day to be buried."*

Social Salvation and the Religious Left Today

King's statement highlights the importance of the social gospel concept of "social salvation" for today's religious left.

Although many of its primary leaders come out of liberal Protestant denominations, the religious left is not a monolithic movement. Its leaders include prominent clergy, such as the Lutheran minister Nadia Boltz-Weber as well as academics such as Cornel West. Some of the movement's major figures, notably

Rev. Jim Wallis, are evangelicals who identify with what is often called progressive evangelicalism.

Others come from outside of Christianity. Rabbi Michael Lerner, founder of the organization Network of Spiritual Progressives, seeks not only to promote interfaith activism but also to attract persons unaffiliated with any religious institutions.

These leaders often focus on different issues. However, they unite around the social gospel belief that religious faith must be committed to the transformation of social structures.

The Network for Spiritual Progressives' mission statement, for example, affirms its desire

> *"To build a social change movement – guided by and infused with spiritual and ethical values – to transform our society to one that prioritizes and promotes the well-being of the people and the planet, as well as love, justice, peace, and compassion over money, power and profit."*

One of the most important voices of the religious left is North Carolina minister William Barber. Barber's organization, "Repairers of the Breach," seeks to train clergy and laity from a variety of faith traditions in grassroots activism. Barber's hope is that grassroots activists will be committed to social change by "rebuilding, raising up and repairing our moral infrastructure."

Other organizations associated with the religious left express similar goals. Often embracing democratic socialism, these groups engage issues of racial justice (including support for the Black Lives Matter movement), LGBT equality and the defense of religious minorities.

An Attractive Option?

Despite the public visibility of activists like Barber, some question whether the religious left can become a potent political force.

Sociologist James Wellman observes that often religious progressives lack the "social infrastructure that creates and sustains a social movement; its leaders are spiritual entrepreneurs rather than institution builders."

Another challenge is the growing secularization of the political left. Only 30 percent of Americans who identify with the political left view religion as a positive force for social change.

At the same time, the religious left's progressive agenda – in particular, its focus on serving society's poor – might be an attractive option for younger Americans who seek alternatives to the perceived dogmatism of the religious right. As an activist connected with Jim Wallis's "Sojourners" organization noted,

> "I think the focus on the person of Jesus is birthing a younger generation.... Their political agenda is shaped by Jesus' call to feed the hungry, make sure the thirsty have clean water, make sure all have access to healthcare, transform America into a welcoming place for immigrants, fix our inequitable penal system, and end abject poverty abroad and in the forgotten corners of our urban and rural communities."

This statement not only circles back to Charles Sheldon's nineteenth century question, "what would Jesus do?" It illustrates, I argue, the continued resiliency of the core social gospel belief in social salvation for a new generation of activists.

Can the religious left achieve the public status of the religious right? The theme of "social salvation" that was critical to Walter Rauschenbusch, A.J. Muste and Martin Luther King Jr. might, I believe, very well galvanize the activism of a new generation of religious progressives.

5

Catholicism and the Tea Party
John Gehring

John Gehring is Catholic Program Director at the organization Faith in Public Life. He is author of The Francis Effect: A Radical Pope's Challenge to the American Catholic Church. *He is a contributing editor at* Commonweal *magazine and an adjunct professor of journalism at American University.*

John Gehring examines contemporary American political issues associated with the far right and the Tea Party movement through the lens of Catholic theology. He argues that the individualistic nature of the movement conflicts with the teachings of the Catholic Church. Gehring draws on the Church's historical opinions regarding taxation and other political issues to support his assertion. Although he points out that a significant percentage of those who identified as Tea Partiers were Catholic, he asserts that these individuals allowed partisanship to overtake morality in a way that was contrary to the Church's teachings.

Tea Party activists elbowed their way into the national media spotlight after the 2008 election with a "Don't Tread on Me" rallying cry that struck familiar themes rooted deep in the American experience. Crowds of flag-waving, self-styled "rugged individualists" told us that they were "Taxed Enough Already" and

---

"The Tea Party and Catholic Social Teaching Don't Mix," by John Gehring, U.S. Catholic. Reprinted by permission.

cast themselves as patriotic defenders of freedom in the revered tradition of Washington, Adams, and Paine.

Despite inflated claims of revolutionary lineage and an undercurrent of racial grievance that has sometimes blemished the Tea Party's image, many political leaders—including GOP presidential candidates Newt Gingrich, Mitt Romney, and Gov. Rick Perry of Texas—embrace this energized movement with the hope of riding a wave of anti-government backlash into the White House. Many Catholics have embraced the movement as well, as a Hart and Associates study found that 28 percent of Tea Partiers identify as Catholic.

Given the Tea Party's rise to prominence and its political success in pushing Republican leaders farther to the right, it's worth examining how the movement's core priorities—particularly on smaller government and fewer taxes—contrast sharply with Catholic values. How should Catholics groomed in a religious tradition that emphasizes the vital role of government and views taxes as a moral responsibility respond to the Tea Party?

Catholics are encouraged to put moral principles before partisanship, and the US bishops' document "Forming Consciences for Faithful Citizenship" has emphasized a broad range of issues for Catholics to consider before voting. The bishops warn against efforts "to reduce Catholic moral concerns to one or two matters, or to justify choices simply to advance partisan, ideological or personal interests."

Catholic Democrats, Republicans and Tea Partiers will all find aspects of Church teaching that challenge their political views in discomforting ways. However, the Tea Party's anti-government rhetoric and emphasis on individualism chafes against Catholic notions of solidarity and a vision for economic justice that seeks to balance personal rights with social responsibilities.

The Tea Party Patriots, one of the largest factions in this decentralized movement, gets straight to the point in its mission statement. "The impetus for the Tea Party movement is excessive government spending and taxation," the statement reads. While no one relishes paying taxes, the Bureau of Economic Analysis reports that federal, state and local income taxes consumed 9.2% of all personal income in 2009, the lowest rate since 1950.

Jesuit priest Father Fred Kammer, a former president of Catholic Charities USA and current president of the Jesuit Social Research Institute in New Orleans, has written that "some 30 years of anti-tax propaganda whose most vociferous current harbinger is the Tea Party" has given many Americans the false impression that they are overtaxed.

In an article for Just South Quarterly, a publication of the Jesuit Social Research Institute, Kammer noted that the United States is one of the lowest-taxed countries in the developed world. Many states also have regressive tax policies that fall hardest on the working poor. Laws that cap property taxes and other sources of municipal revenue often erode the capacity to fund public schools, transportation and social-safety nets that protect the most vulnerable. These tax policies contribute to "a widening of the gap between rich and poor to its currently morally grotesque levels and the substantial deterioration of the U.S. infrastructure," Kammer wrote.

The non-partisan Congressional Budget Office released a widely covered report in October that found the top 1 percent of earners more than doubled their share of the nation's earnings over the last three decades. The report shows that over the last 30 years a greater tax burden has fallen on middle and working class Americans.

Tax policies that contribute to the most extreme gap between rich and poor since the Great Depression have inspired billionaires like Warren Buffet and Bill Gates to call for higher taxes on the wealthy, a view supported by most Americans according to numerous surveys. The 400 wealthiest Americans now have a greater combined net worth than the bottom 150 million Americans. Buffet and Gates are not the only ones raising alarms.

In his 2008 encyclical, *Caritas in Veritate*, Pope Benedict XVI denounced the "scandal of glaring inequalities" and called for a more just distribution of wealth.

The Catholic approach to taxes and government often cuts against prevailing political and cultural winds. In Catholic terms, paying taxes is part of our collective responsibility for the common good. "The tax system should be continually evaluated in terms of its impact on the poor," the US Catholic bishops wrote in Economic Justice for All, a 1986 pastoral letter that echoes the teaching of several popes.

The bishops called for a more progressive tax system "so that those with relatively greater financial resources pay a higher rate of taxation." Last October, US bishops wrote a letter to lawmakers noting that "too often the weak and vulnerable are not heard in the tax debate," and urged Congress to preserve the Child Tax Credit and the Earned Income Tax Credit that help many low-income Americans avoid falling below the poverty line.

In his encyclical, *Mater et Magistra*, Pope John XXIII wrote that "as regards taxation, assessment according to the ability to pay is fundamental to a just and equitable system." Pope John Paul II, while embraced by many conservatives, was also a bold critic of unregulated capitalism who warned against an "idolatry of the market" and insisted that private wealth was subject to a "social mortgage."

Compare this insistence on a sound ethical foundation for economic policies with the priorities of some presidential candidates and political leaders who support tax policies that most economists say would cut taxes for the wealthiest one percent of Americans without benefiting struggling workers.

For example, Newt Gingrich, Gov. Rick Perry and former GOP presidential hopeful Herman Cain (who still plays a visible role as a political commentator) have all proposed versions of a "flax tax" often embraced by Tea Party supporters. Despite its egalitarian sounding name, this method of taxation falls hardest on the poor and working families, according to most economists and analysis from the non-partisan Tax Policy Center in Washington.

Debates over taxes and size of government have also been influenced by a network of Washington "think tanks" and prominent figures on Capitol Hill. Washington anti-tax lobbyist Grover Norquist, president of Americans for Tax Reform, has long been a powerful force in conservative politics with a "starve the beast" approach to defunding government. Most Republican members of Congress (and 3 Democrats) have endorsed his "Tax Payer Protection" pledge, which according to Norquist's lobbying organization prohibits lawmakers from supporting "any and all tax increases." Norquist once remarked that it was his goal to reduce the size of the federal government to the point where it could be "drowned in a bathtub."

While Republicans have led the charge for lower taxes on the wealthy in recent decades, leading Democrats have also fought hard to keep capital gains taxes low even as they criticize the GOP for tax policies that coddle the rich. Seeking to find compromises with a Republican-controlled Congress in the 1990s, Bill Clinton cut the capital gains tax rate, which disproportionately benefits a small minority of elite investors.

President Barack Obama, pressured by Republicans during debt negotiations, agreed to maintain Bush-era tax cuts for the rich in exchange for an extension of unemployment benefits conservatives wanted to end. When President Obama last fall proposed a deficit reduction plan funded in part by closing tax loopholes for corporations and ending Bush tax cuts for those making more than $200,000 a year, conservative political leaders, including Catholic Rep. Paul Ryan of Wisconsin, accused him of engaging in "class warfare."

Ryan appears to draw the wrong lessons from his Church's teachings on economic justice and failed to mention that the 400 richest Americans now own more wealth than the bottom half of Americans combined.

The principles of just taxation encouraged by the Catholic social tradition are rooted in a positive vision for government and a healthy skepticism of unbridled markets. The radical individualism and anti-government ideology espoused by the Tea Party simply don't fit with Catholic communitarian values and Gospel commands to care for our neighbors, especially the poor and vulnerable.

Church officials are unlikely to show up at a rally any time soon, but if they do, it's safe to say you're more likely to find Pope Benedict XVI standing in solidarity with Occupy Wall Street protestors than Tea Party activists.

6

Not All Scientists Are Atheists

Amy McCaig

Amy McCaig is a senior media relations specialist in the Office of Public Affairs at Rice University. She is a prolific writer with a broad range of experience in the communications and public relations sphere.

In this viewpoint, Amy McCaig examines polling data related to the popular belief that scientists are generally hostile to religion, a conception that figures prominently in debates about religious and science education. McCaig argues that in reality many scientists identify as religious, and that only a small percentage of scientists believe science and faith to be in conflict. The data is drawn from regions around the world and looks at patterns of belief among scientists in various regional contexts.

Are all scientists atheists? Do they believe religion and science can co-exist? These questions and others were addressed in the first worldwide survey of how scientists view religion, released today by researchers at Rice University.

"No one today can deny that there is a popular 'warfare' framing between science and religion," said the study's principal investigator, Elaine Howard Ecklund, founding director of Rice University's Religion and Public Life Program and the Herbert

Amy McCaig, "First Worldwide Survey of Religion and Science: No, Not All Scientists Are Atheists," Copyright © December 03, 2015 by SAGE Publications, Inc. Reprinted by permission of SAGE Publications, Inc.

S. Autrey Chair in Social Sciences. "This is a war of words fueled by scientists, religious people and those in between."

The study's results challenge longstanding assumptions about the science-faith interface. While it is commonly assumed that most scientists are atheists, the global perspective resulting from the study shows that this is simply not the case.

"More than half of scientists in India, Italy, Taiwan and Turkey self-identify as religious," Ecklund said. "And it's striking that approximately twice as many 'convinced atheists' exist in the general population of Hong Kong, for example, (55 percent) compared with the scientific community in this region (26 percent)."

The researchers did find that scientists are generally less religious than a given general population. However, there were exceptions to this: 39 percent of scientists in Hong Kong identify as religious compared with 20 percent of the general population of Hong Kong, and 54 percent of scientists in Taiwan identify as religious compared with 44 percent of the general population of Taiwan. Ecklund noted that such patterns challenge longstanding assumptions about the irreligious character of scientists around the world.

When asked about terms of conflict between religion and science, Ecklund noted that only a minority of scientists in each regional context believe that science and religion are in conflict. In the UK—one of the most secular countries studied—only 32 percent of scientists characterized the science-faith interface as one of conflict. In the US, this number was only 29 percent. And 25 percent of Hong Kong scientists, 27 percent of Indian scientists, and 23 percent of Taiwanese scientists believed science and religion can coexist and be used to help each other.

In addition to the survey's quantitative findings, the researchers found nuanced views in scientists' responses during interviews. For example, numerous scientists expressed how religion can provide a "check" in ethically gray areas.

"(Religion provides a) check on those occasions where you might be tempted to shortcut because you want to get something published and you think, 'Oh, that experiment wasn't really good enough, but if I portray it in this way, that will do,'" said a biology professor from the UK.

Another scientist said that there are "multiple atheisms," some of which include religious traditions.

"I have no problem going to church services because quite often, again that's a cultural thing," said a physics reader in the UK who said he sometimes attended services because his daughter sang in the church choir. "It's like looking at another part of your culture, but I have no faith religiously. It doesn't worry me that religion is still out there."

Finally, many scientists mentioned ways that they would accommodate the religious views or practices of the public, whether those of students or colleagues.

"Religious issues (are) quite common here because everyone talks about which temple they go to, which church they go to. So it's not really an issue we hide; we just talk about it. Because, in Taiwan, we have people [of] different religions," said a Taiwanese professor of biology.

Ecklund and fellow Rice researchers Kirstin Matthews and Steven Lewis collected information from 9,422 respondents in eight regions around the world: France, Hong Kong, India, Italy, Taiwan, Turkey, the UK and the US They also traveled to these regions to conduct in-depth interviews with 609 scientists, the largest worldwide survey and interview study ever conducted of the intersection between faith and science.

By surveying and interviewing scientists at various career stages, in elite and nonelite institutions and in biology and physics, the researchers hoped to gain a representative look at scientists' views on religion, ethics and how both intersect with their scientific work.

Ecklund said that the study has many important implications that can be applied to university hiring processes, how classrooms and labs are structured and general public policy.

"Science is a global endeavor," Ecklund said. "And as long as science is global, then we need to recognize that the borders between science and religion are more permeable than most people think."

The Templeton World Charity Foundation funded the study. The study also received support from Rice University and the Faraday Institute, housed at St. Edmund's College, Cambridge.

7

Topeka and the Westboro Baptist Church

Southern Poverty Law Center

The Southern Poverty Law Center is dedicated to fighting hate and bigotry and to seeking justice for the most vulnerable members of our society. Using litigation, education, and other forms of advocacy, the SPLC works toward the day when the ideals of equal justice and equal opportunity will be a reality.

This viewpoint examines the history of the Westboro Baptist Church, a conservative congregation in Topeka, Kansas, notorious for its provocative protests against homosexuality. The group pressures politicians and community leaders to succumb to their influence, attempting to force out those who might oppose the group. Through various means of coercion the church has managed to assert influence over Topeka politics, but there have also been attempts to combat it, with local and state laws passed to help keep them in check.

No one says that Fred Waldron Phelps, Sr., or his congregation at the Westboro Baptist Church (WBC) are any friends of the Topeka police department. For years, police listened as complaints streamed in that WBC's picketers, with signs reading "God Hates F-gs" and "F-gs Die/God Laughs," went beyond the bounds of free speech.

They took reports from people who were battered, harassed, stalked and spat on by the Westboro congregants. They heard about scores of people like the mainstream preacher who was

"Topeka: A City Bulled into Submission by the Westboro Baptist Church," Southern Poverty Law Center. Reprinted by permission.

accused by one of Phelps' followers of — "drink[ing] anal blood at the altar of the sphincter."

Still, Fred Phelps and the police found ways to get along — perhaps a little too well. The city's police chief was asked to resign in 1997 after allegedly instructing his officers never to arrest Phelps or his picketing congregants.

The new chief, who had tangled with Phelps earlier, promised to stand up to the man, to end the special treatment. Within months, Phelps and his lawyer-laden church had written up 40 pages of complaints and sued him.

To settle the case, the chief promised to never publicly discuss Phelps or deal personally with his church. Today, it is a brave local indeed who dares to stand up to the man who may be America's most vitriolic fountain of anti-homosexual hate.

"They have used their constitutional rights," Topeka Mayor Joan Wagnon says of Phelps and his followers, "to bully this town into submission."

For 10 years, Phelps and his Westboro Baptists — a congregation almost entirely composed of his extended family — have waged a battle against lesbians, gays and a whole host of other perceived enemies.

They have used daily pickets, an array of intimidating tactics, scores of lawsuits and a veritable flood of faxes that are so filled with slurs and sex that they rival the product of the most prolific professional pornographer.

They run America's most infamous anti-homosexual web site, www.godhatesf-gs.com. In the process, even as they made life miserable for their enemies, Fred Phelps and his followers have created a niche for themselves in Topeka.

And if, as some say, the city and church have grown more tolerant of one another in recent years, credit may be due as much to Phelps' intimidation as to any success by the city or its inhabitants in leashing his mad-dog tactics.

"Topeka is now identified with Fred Phelps," a chagrined Mayor Wagnon said in an interview with the *Intelligence Report*.

"If someone could figure out how to get him off the streets, they could be elected mayor for life."

'A Human Abuse Machine'

The Westboro Baptist Church is most famous — or infamous — for its campaign against homosexuality. Its members have traveled from San Francisco to Canada to New Hampshire preaching "the Bible's hatred," advocating the death penalty for homosexuals and picketing the funerals of gay AIDS and murder victims, most visibly that of Matthew Shepard in Wyoming.

[…]

All concerned agree that the WBC really does hate gays. But at least one church member has said openly that if all homosexuals disappeared, congregants would find some other reason to picket.

And Suzanne James, who recently resigned after eight years in the Shawnee County District Attorney's office as director of victim services, says Phelps's opposition to homosexuality obscures a deeper purpose — promoting himself and hurting others.

"I'm so tired of people calling him an 'anti-gay activist,'" James told the *Report*. "He's not an anti-gay activist. He's a human abuse machine."

The most striking aspect of Westboro Baptist pickets is the relentlessly personal nature of their taunts. Their targets are only sometimes homosexuals; as often as not, they are simply people who somehow crossed the Phelpses, often unintentionally.

WBC members have picketed the funerals of Bill Clinton's mother, Sonny Bono and Frank Sinatra. Even Bob Dole, Jerry Falwell, the Ku Klux Klan, Santa Claus and the 17 sailors killed aboard the U.S.S. Cole in Yemen last October have been attacked as "f-gs" or "supporters of the f-g agenda."

One little girl, going with her parents to see the "Nutcracker" ballet in a Topeka hall, had WBC pickets hiss at her: "Did your Daddy stick in his p---k in your a-- last night?"

Typically, targets are Topeka locals, whose names are memorialized in lurid WBC picket signs protesting "F-g Meneley" (for former sheriff Dave Meneley), "Bull D-ke James" (Suzanne James), "Jo-ANus Hamilton" (Shawnee County District Attorney Joan Hamilton). Once the signs are made, the WBC congregants go to work.

For 10 Years, '40 Pickets a Week'

They picket people at their offices, at the restaurants they patronize, in the schools their children attend. They picket church services, beauty pageants, basketball games, even "Peace Camps" for young kids. They picket weddings and they picket funerals. In Topeka, they have picketed the courthouses, the city's newspaper, a local university and almost every other church in town.

They have picketed people at their homes, while they prepared for work in the morning or threw parties at night. They hated one Nissan car dealer enough to drive 500 miles and picket the Nissan factory in Smyrna, Tenn.

In an interview with the *Report,* Fred Phelps estimated that since 1991, WBC has carried out 40 pickets a week, every week. What's remarkable is that he may not be exaggerating by much.

"There was a woman working at my restaurant who was gay," says Jerry Berger, an attorney and owner of Topeka's Vintage Restaurant. "Phelps told me, 'If you don't fire her, we're going to put you out of business.'" The Westboro Baptists proceeded to picket the restaurant "literally every day" for about three years. Berger eventually sold the restaurant and the woman quit.

Phelps didn't. He followed the unfortunate woman, picketing at her new job, and "he still pickets the restaurant all the time," Berger said in a recent interview. "And now, he pickets my law offices every Tuesday."

The Cost of Courage

The Phelpses don't just picket, they also fax. And what faxes. Sent out to dozens of government offices, law firms, businesses and homes across Kansas several times a week, the faxes are grotesque, non-stop political commentary lambasting local and national figures.

Minnesota Sen. Paul Wellstone is a "bug-eye f-ggy baby-killer." Sailors in the US Navy are "blasphemous f-g beasts." Jerry Berger, the Vintage owner, is a "[B]loody Jew... merchant of anal copulating."

Joe Lieberman, Al Gore's Democratic running mate last fall, is "an anti-Christ Jew" who "has sold his soul to f-gs." Elizabeth Taylor is "an evil woman" who led a "wicked, Christ-rejecting, Satan-worshipping life." Jesse Jackson is a "f-g" and a "black Judas goat leading his people to hell."

Thanksgiving was established as a "pagan feast" so the Massachusetts governor could "lust after the semi-naked bodies of the Indians he invited." Poet Maya Angelou is the "filthy face of f-g evil."

Some of these faxes are reproduced on www.godhatesf-gs.com, the WBC web site.

And then there are the lawsuits. Phelps himself is a disbarred attorney who was long known for massive litigation; at one point, he personally had almost 200 lawsuits pending in federal court. Although his congregation includes only about 22 adults, at least 14 of those have law degrees.

The church has its own law firm, Phelps Chartered, which is staffed by church members and which has repeatedly filed suit against its perceived enemies.

In addition to suing the chief of police and various Kansas judges and politicians, it has sued one district attorney three times for "malicious prosecution." Even private citizens who filed criminal complaints against the picketers found themselves embroiled in lawsuits — or, perhaps by coincidence, with roofing nails littering their driveways.

"We should stand up and be counted against this hatred, but I can recognize a moral dilemma to being courageous," concedes Randy Austin, former head of the Concerned Citizens of Topeka, a group established to counter WBC.

I can hold myself up for the picketing, the lawsuits, the harassment," says Austin, a lawyer who manages a trust that owns shopping centers. "But what if I stand up to them and they put one of my tenants out of business? That's not okay."

Hate as a Family Value

The 50-odd adult and juvenile members of the Westboro Baptist Church are almost exclusively the extended family, by blood or marriage, of Fred Phelps, Sr.

Although four of his 13 children are estranged from Phelps and the church, nine — all attorneys — remain loyal. Most of those live on or near the same city block that holds their church.

Phelps' property and his residence, including a large swimming pool that he describes as a "baptismal font," are tax-exempt. Institutionally, WBC is an independent Baptist church that is not formally affiliated with any other Baptist denomination — although Topeka's mainline Baptist churches are apparently the only churches in Topeka that have failed to condemn WBC'S astounding vitriol.

According to tree if the Phelps children who are estranged from their father, the church's behavior is part of their father's long history of conflict. They tell of a family whose profound insularity may explain why the church today does virtually no recruiting.

With a great deal of detail, they allege that their father engaged in physical and emotional abuse of his children, reflecting a need for control that bordered on brainwashing. All three claim that at home he referred to black people as "dumb n--gers."

"He behaves with a viciousness the likes of which I have never seen [elsewhere]," wrote one estranged son, Mark Phelps, who described his father as "a small, pathetic, old man."

"My father is a very unstable person who is determined to hurt people. ... I believe it's a good idea to respond to him with caution much like the caution used when dealing with a rattlesnake or a mad dog."

A Decade of Trouble

"He only started picketing in 1991, but I want people to understand that nothing's changed, he's been like this all along," adds Dortha Bird, a daughter of Phelps who is now a practicing lawyer in Topeka. Bird legally changed her last name when she left her family because, she says, she felt "free as a bird."

For 10 years now, Phelps has treated this city of 150,000 in much the same way as he allegedly treated his own children. It was in 1991 that he started "The Great Gage Park Decency Drive," pickets aimed at ending an alleged epidemic of homosexual sex in a park.

During the course of those and other pickets, Phelps and his followers engaged in activities that resulted in battery, criminal restraint and disorderly conduct convictions.

But convictions have been the exception. Of the hundreds of criminal complaints against WBC picketers lodged with police, at least 109 were forwarded to the district attorney's office, a large proportion of them against Phelps and one son, Jonathan. Only four cases resulted in convictions.

These figures give some idea of the harassment Topekans face at the hands of Phelps and his followers. But there are uncounted ugly incidents which did not involve any alleged criminality. Mayor Wagnon remembers the computer supplier who had to walk past a Phelps picket line on his way into her office.

"He stood there shaking, obviously emotionally devastated, and I asked him what was wrong," Wagnon said. "He said, 'My son committed suicide three weeks ago because he was gay. How can you let them stand there like that?'"

Sex and Politics in Topeka

Very few in Topeka — a highly conservative town in a highly conservative state — admit to being allies of Fred Phelps or the WBC. Yet many are sympathetic to Phelps' anti-homosexual message, even if they find his tactics repulsive.

In 1990, the year before Phelps started his Gage Park picketing, he ran as a Democrat in the Kansas gubernatorial primary and won 6.7% of the vote.

In 1992, after one year of publicly flaunting his hatred of homosexuals, Phelps' popularity had actually shot up dramatically: He polled 31% of the vote in the Kansas Democratic primary for US Senate, taking about 50,000 ballots. Last November, without even running for office, Phelps received write-in votes for several local offices.

But Phelps' influence goes deeper. Fearing WBC harassment, some state legislators refused to vote against Kansas' apparently unconstitutional criminal sodomy statute, says Mayor Wagnon. When the Topeka Human Relations Commission later decided merely to examine issues facing local gays and lesbians, the city council reacted by abolishing the commission.

According to commissioner Richard Alexander, the council feared Phelps' reaction. (After a public outcry, the commission was reestablished, but in a weakened form.) And because of Phelps' diatribes, city officials say, Topeka restricted public comment at city council meetings and declined a public access television channel.

Even more heavy-handed tactics are also common.

According to Jerry Palmer, an attorney involved in various legal conflicts with WBC, the city council passed an ordinance in the early 1990s that would have restricted pickets during church services and funerals. The measure required only the signature of then-Mayor Butch Felker in order to become law.

"Then a fax came out saying something like, 'The mayor has been playing around in the fleshpots of Parks and Recreation. No names yet but stay tuned,'" says Palmer. "We all regarded that as a tacit threat that Phelps would publicly reveal the name of Felker's extramarital girlfriend, who worked at the local zoo."

Felker, who later married the woman, vetoed the proposed law, telling constituents it was unconstitutional.

Spilling Secrets

People who cross the Westboro Baptists have consistently had their unfortunate secrets spread around town. District Attorney Hamilton, who had run on a promise to stand up to the picketers, thought it was bad enough that she was repeatedly sued and that picketers would scream "p---ks go up your a--" as she passed by with her elderly parents.

But then she woke up one morning to find that a private e-mail she had written to her husband, discussing both of their adulterous relationships, had been faxed to offices across the city.

City councilwoman Beth Listrom had confidential blood records describing her exposure to hepatitis faxed around on Westboro Baptist letterhead. The fax said Listrom was "tainted with a social disease (in the genre of AIDS or HIV+)."

Both the e-mail and the medical records apparently had been retrieved from the trash.

But even these remarkable tactics haven't turned off all local officials. A number seem to remain on remarkably friendly terms with Pastor Phelps.

Current City Councilman James McClinton, a black man who has been portrayed as a monkey in several faxes of unknown origin, alleges other council members and officials routinely leak sensitive information to Phelps. Within hours of many closed-door executive sessions of the council, he says, Phelps has learned the details and, in some cases, faxed them all over town.

Shawnee County Treasurer Rita Cline is a declared sympathizer. Describing Phelps as "a great civil rights leader" for lawsuits he won before being disbarred, she denies he has received special treatment from local officials. "If anything," she told the *Report*, "they've mistreated him."

Cline, who calls homosexuality "sinful" and tolerance of gays "garbage," disavows any special ties to Phelps. But Phelps is not so retiring. "We're the ones," he says, "who convinced her to run."

In any event, Cline is far from seeing Phelps as a blight upon Topeka. "I highly respect the gentleman," she declares. "How could you not?"

The Price of Hate

For years, economic growth in Topeka has been negligible — a dilemma Westboro Baptist has clearly helped to exacerbate. But the Topeka Convention and Visitor's Bureau (CVB), which promotes city tourism and economic development, has declined to investigate the problem.

According to Randy Austin and Betty Simecka, who are both former CVB presidents, that is because of fear of Phelps' harassment. Frustrated, Simecka and another former CVB employee got together privately to document the effect of Phelps and his church on convention business.

They found five instances where lost conventions could be directly attributed to WBC'S activities. In one case, a potential convention client was touring the city with a CVB official when they drove by a Phelps picket. "The lady [client] was hysterical and got down on the floor of the car," the Simecka report said. "They will not ever consider Topeka for a meeting 'as long as the Phelps group has a presence.'"

The estimated loss in these cases alone was $16.5 million.

Other impacts are harder to quantify. Picketers have routinely frightened spectators away from the city's money-losing Performing Arts Center. Poet Maya Angelou — who wrote and delivered a poem at President Clinton's inauguration — was so shaken when she spoke at the center that she cancelled her remaining Kansas appearances.

Even hiring city staff has gotten harder. Once, Mayor Wagnon drove by a Phelps picket shortly after giving a job to an openly gay city planner. Turning to the mayor, he told her he could never live in the same city as Phelps.

In the end, it was these kinds of economic costs that led to the creation in 1995 of the Concerned Citizens of Topeka (CCT), a citizens group that has grown into the most effective organization to take on Phelps and his family. Lobbying by CCT'S 800 members helped widen the picket-free zone around church services.

It prompted officials to put the church's pickup truck back on the tax rolls (WBC had argued that the truck, which carried picket signs like "F-g Dole" in reference to Sen. Bob Dole of Kansas, was used exclusively for "religious" purposes). And CCT helped to spark a revealing 1997 investigation of the police chief of Topeka.

Tolerating Intolerance

In the mid-1990s, Topeka had both a mayor and a police chief who were seen by many as sympathetic to Phelps, men who agreed that homosexuality is a sin.

Chief Gerald Beavers already was facing some public criticism for assigning contingents of police to the Phelps pickets — not to protect passersby, but to guard the *picketers*. Later, he would be accused of coddling Phelps in other ways.

This reported coddling had its effect. Gene Roles, whose sisters experienced "absolute physical devastation" from a screaming attack by Jonathan Phelps, likened their experience to "verbal rape." Roles says that the biggest hurdle in eventually convicting Jonathan Phelps of disorderly conduct in that incident came from an unexpected quarter — the Topeka Police Department.

"They all said they had been briefed not to issue reports on the Phelpses," Roles told the *Intelligence Report*. "We talked to 10 officers and got 10 different reasons why. In the end, winning the case came down to simply following through on a police report. The jury was convinced in 15 minutes."

A few years later, officers came forward to essentially corroborate the Roles story, complaining publicly that they'd been instructed by Beavers not to arrest members of the Phelps family.

Beavers denied that charge, although Fred Phelps says today that the two men "understood each other." In any event, then-Mayor Felker says he told Beavers to resign or face firing. Beavers quit.

Speechless in Topeka

Dean Forster, the current chief, came in with what were seen as strong Phelps-fighting credentials. Phelps Chartered had been forced to pay Forster many thousands of dollars in legal fees after a judge ruled that a Phelps civil rights suit against Forster was frivolous.

But Forster was soon sued again by the Phelpses, and as part of a settlement the police department agreed in writing to allow only five Topeka officers — not including Forster — to deal with WBC. Department officials say Forster also verbally agreed not to publicly discuss the church or the Phelpses.

For some, the new administration has changed little.

Bridget Newman was 16 in the summer of 1999, when she says she was "verbally attacked" by Jonathan Phelps on the street. She and her mother contacted the police. "When we told the police officer we wanted to press charges, he smiled and said, 'Oh, you must be from out of town. The Phelpses just do these things and there's nothing we can do about it. It's within their legal rights,'" Bridget recalls.

"I turned away crying and really upset. They had all the rights and I had none."

The Newmans ultimately did file a report. But Bridget says a Topeka detective called her mother a short time later. "He advised us not to press charges and said they could make our lives hell, that we didn't know what they could do."

A hearing in the case has been postponed indefinitely.

Police official Ed Klumpp — one of the five officers allowed to publicly discuss WBC — says officials can do little other than police the pickets for violence or other lawbreaking. In fact, Klumpp says he often recommends that communities facing Phelps pickets concentrate on preventing potential violence from counter-demonstrators.

But retired detective Doug Mauck disagrees, saying officials could do things like separate picketers from their targets. "If we had been alert in 1991 and known where it was going," he laments today, "we could have stopped in then and there. Law enforcement could have been a big help."

Fighting Back

In some ways, the raw vitriol peddled by the Westboro Baptist Church has had some positive effects. There have been years of counterpickets, meetings, street fairs, fundraisers, rallies and invited speakers. Many targeted churches have joined together to proclaim that "God's Love Speaks Loudest."

And last spring, the city council unanimously passed a resolution condemning hate — although even that mild document prompted as yet unfulfilled threats of retaliatory lawsuits.

Even some local homosexuals say Phelps has managed to unite the city in unexpected ways. "Phelps has actually been good for Topeka and for the gay community," says J.L. Cleland. "Topekans would rather sweep problems of race and sexual orientation under the carpet. Now, they can't do that."

State laws passed in the early 1990s — mainly as a response to Phelps — regulate funeral picketing, stalking and fax machine harassment. City ordinances now limit the picketing of private residences and church services.

Today, in the wake of the handful of criminal convictions of picketers, some say there have been noticeable, if mild, changes in WBC'S behavior. In Topeka, members don't scream as much at passersby — although they still do in other states. Complaints to police and Phelps lawsuits have slowed as WBC'S efforts have shifted to the national scene.

One local lawyer, Pedro Irigonegaray, came up with a novel way to battle the Phelpses. When Phelps Chartered, alleging "emotional damage," sued someone who had filed a criminal complaint against a WBC member, Irigonegaray's team requested court approval to have a psychiatrist evaluate Phelps family members to determine the alleged damage. The Phelps firm settled without delay.

For his part, Fred Phelps, holding one of his church's 800 picket signs, says he's gone "way past 'hate' to 'detest,' 'abhor.'" He pauses, searching for the right words for his enemies. "All they think about day and night is fornicating."

Well, maybe. Many people have speculated about Phelps' desperate hatred of homosexuals, wondering if he has something to hide.

"There's only one person in this town who thinks about homosexual fornication day and night," says Richard Alexander, the former human relations commissioner who is also a member of Topeka's Gay and Lesbian Task Force. "And he's not in our task force."

In the end, the city of Topeka may yet get the better of Phelps, a man who many in this Kansas city think of as the demented uncle best left locked away in an upstairs bedroom.

"If there's one thing we've learned through all of this," Suzanne James concludes, "it's that you can only beat a bully by standing up to him."

8

Supreme Court Rules in Favor of Westboro Baptist Church
Nina Totenberg

Nina Totenberg is NPR's award-winning legal affairs correspondent. Her reports air regularly on NPR's critically acclaimed newsmagazines All Things Considered, Morning Edition, and Weekend Edition. Totenberg's coverage of the Supreme Court and legal affairs has won her widespread recognition.

Nina Totenberg reports on the US Supreme Court's 8-1 decision to shield the Westboro Baptist Church from liability for emotional damage caused by their protesting of military funerals. This decision upholds the First Amendment right to freedom of expression, including of a controversial or religious nature. However, the court did not address state laws intended to create buffer zones of 100 feet around funerals to prevent protests, leaving the question open for further discussion in the future.

The US Supreme Court has ruled that protesters at military funerals cannot be sued for inflicting emotional distress on the family of a dead soldier. The vote was 8 to 1.

When Marine Lance Cpl. Matthew Snyder was killed in Iraq, his funeral in Westminster, Md., drew thousands to pay their respects. But it also drew a protest from the Rev. Fred Phelps

©2011 National Public Radio, Inc. NPR news report "High Court Rules for Anti-Gay Protesters at Funerals" by Nina Totenberg as originally published on npr.org on March 2, 2011, and is used with the permission of NPR. Any unauthorized duplication is strictly prohibited.

The Role of Religion in Public Policy

and six other members of the Westboro Baptist Church, based in Topeka, Kan.

Phelps and other church members have traveled the country for years, picketing hundreds of military funerals to communicate their belief that "God hates the USA" for its tolerance of homosexuality, particularly in the military.

The picketers did not contend that Snyder was gay. Rather, their message, as Phelps puts it, was that "the whole country is given over to sodomy and to sodomite enablers."

The picketers followed their usual practice at the Snyder funeral. They alerted police in advance and followed instructions to set up their protest on public property, at a site 1,000 feet away from the church, near the vehicle entrance.

Though the protest was peaceful and ended before the funeral began, the picketers carried signs with messages offensive to many, including "Thank God for Dead Soldiers," "F-gs Doom Nations" and "America Is Doomed."

Albert Snyder, the father of the dead Marine, did not see the signs until later when he viewed TV coverage. He says the picketers turned his son's funeral into a circus, taking away his "last moment" with his son.

"This was a funeral. This wasn't a parade going down the street. I shouldn't have to look away from anything at my own child's funeral," Snyder says. "That's absurd."

Snyder sued Phelps and his church for intentional infliction of emotional distress.

"These people targeted me and my family, and they have done this to over 200 other military men and women's families," Snyder says, his voice rising. "I want to know how you would feel if somebody stood 30 feet away from the main vehicle entrance of a church where you're trying to bury your mother, with a sign that says, 'Thank God for dead sluts.' You tell me that shouldn't be illegal. Is 'f-g' any worse than 'slut'?"

A jury agreed with Snyder and awarded him $5 million in damages. But the Supreme Court set aside that verdict Wednesday.

Writing for the court majority, Chief Justice John Roberts said that as repugnant as many of the signs were, they were still plainly related to public, rather than private, matters. They focused on "the political and moral conduct of the United States and its citizens," he said, and speech of such public concern is protected by the First Amendment.

Although Westboro may have chosen to protest the funeral to gain publicity for its views, said the chief justice, and although those views may be particularly hurtful to the dead soldier's father, that does not mean the church members' right of free speech can be curtailed or punished. And a jury award amounts to punishment, Roberts contended, by imposing a penalty for expressing an unpopular viewpoint.

"Speech is powerful," Roberts said in conclusion. "It can stir people to action, move them to tears of both joy and sorrow, and — as it did here — inflict great pain. On the facts before us, we cannot react to that pain by punishing the speaker. As a nation we have chosen a different course — to protect even hurtful speech on public issues to ensure that we do not stifle public debate."

Reaction to the decision was markedly muted, given the outrage voiced by veterans groups and politicians at the time the case was argued in the Supreme Court.

The Democratic and Republican leaders of the Senate, along with 40 other members of Congress, filed a brief on Snyder's side. But on Wednesday, reaction on Capitol Hill was nowhere to be found, except in a couple of written statements.

Lawyer Gene Schaerr, who filed a brief in the case for the American Legion, said he was heartened by the fact that the court specifically mentioned that 43 states have enacted laws that put a buffer zone of 100 feet or more around funeral sites. Such laws would not have affected the protest in this case, since protesters were 1,000 feet away.

Nonetheless, says Schaerr, the decision "sends a clear signal to the lower courts that they should not interpret anything in this opinion as casting any doubt about those statutes." The court, however, specifically left open that question, noting that restrictions on the time, place and manner of protests are appropriate in some circumstances.

Wednesday's 8-to-1 ruling came as no surprise to First Amendment scholars, both right and left. They note that the decision is in line with many court decisions protecting the rights of fringe groups — from Nazis marching in Skokie, Ill., to flag burners at a Republican convention in Texas.

University of Chicago law professor Geoffrey Stone notes that Wednesday's ruling fits neatly into that tradition, calling it a "classic case." The only surprise, maintained Stone, was that anyone dissented.

Justice Samuel Alito was the lone dissenter. He viewed the protesters' speech as targeting a private person — the father of the dead soldier — and said that the First Amendment does not give license to such outrageous conduct.

"In order to have a society in which public issues can be openly and vigorously debated," wrote Alito, "it is not necessary to allow the brutalization of innocent victims."

9

The Social and Legal Dimensions of the US Evolution Debate

David Masci

David Masci is a senior writer and editor at the Pew Research Center, where he is the in-house expert on church-state issues, culture war issues, and religion and science. Masci has a bachelor's in medieval history from Syracuse University and a JD from the George Washington University Law School.

In this viewpoint, David Masci examines the history of religious perspectives on the theory of evolution in the United States and how controversy in this area has impacted the politics of public education. While the theory was widely debated in intellectual circles as early as the late nineteenth century, its place in school curricula only came into question with the Scopes trial of 1925. Over time, the question of how evolution should be taught in public schools or whether it should be taught at all has generated many responses.

As with many social and political controversies in the United States, the battle over evolution has been largely fought in courtrooms. This has been particularly true in the last 50 years, as courts have been repeatedly asked to rule on efforts to restrict or change the way public schools teach about evolution and life's origins.

"The Social and Legal Dimensions of the Evolution Debate in the U.S." by David Masci, Pew Research Center, February 3, 2014. Reprinted by permission.

Ironically, when Charles Darwin's evolutionary theory was first made public in the United States almost 150 years ago, it did not roil the country's religious and scientific establishments as it did in Britain at the time. Indeed, while the 1859 publication of *On the Origin of Species by Means of Natural Selection* generated debate among American scientists and thinkers, it was largely ignored by the nation's wider society, due, at least in part, to the country's preoccupation with the Civil War, slavery and, later, Reconstruction.

Still, by the 1870s, American religious leaders and thinkers began considering the theological implications of Darwin's theory, and many started attacking evolutionary thinking. For example, Presbyterian theologian Charles Hodge, in his book *What Is Darwinism?* (1874), argued that natural selection was unacceptable because it directly contradicted belief in a benevolent and all-powerful God. Other theologians, however, such as famed Congregationalist minister Henry Ward Beecher, tried to forge a rapprochement between evolutionary thinking and Christianity, arguing that evolution was simply God's method of creation.

But these early debates over faith and evolution, while important, were largely confined to intellectual circles. The issue did not filter down to the wider American public until the end of the 19th century, when a large number of popular Christian authors and speakers, including the famed Chicago evangelist and missionary Dwight L. Moody, began to inveigh against Darwinism as a threat to biblical truth and public morality.

The arrival of Darwinian thinking into the wider American consciousness coincided with other dramatic shifts taking place in the country's religious landscape. From the 1890s to the 1930s, the major American Protestant denominations – which, in spite of growing doctrinal differences, had generally maintained unity on basic issues of faith – gradually split into two camps: modernist, or theologically liberal Protestantism; and evangelical, or otherwise theologically conservative, Protestantism.

The Social and Legal Dimensions of the US Evolution Debate

The American Protestant schism was caused by a number of important developments taking place at the time, including the advent of new scientific thinking, new questions about the historical accuracy of biblical accounts and a host of provocative and controversial new ideas about both the individual and society associated with such thinkers as Sigmund Freud and Karl Marx. Modernist Protestants sought to integrate these new theories and ideas into their religious doctrine, while more conservative Protestants and others resisted these developments.

By the early 1920s, evolution had become one of the most, if not the most, important wedge issues in this Protestant divide, in part because the debate had taken on a pedagogical dimension, with students throughout the nation now studying Darwin's ideas in biology classes. Not surprisingly, the issue became a mainstay for Protestant evangelists, including Billy Sunday, the most popular preacher of his era. "I don't believe the old bastard theory of evolution," he exclaimed during a 1925 revival meeting in Memphis, Tenn. "I believe I am just as God Almighty made me," he said. But it was William Jennings Bryan, a man of politics, not the cloth, who ultimately became the leader of a full-fledged national crusade against evolution.

Bryan, a populist orator and devout evangelical Protestant who had thrice run unsuccessfully for president, believed that the presence of Darwin in the nation's classrooms would result in the moral destruction of American youth. He argued that the teaching of evolution would ensure that whole generations would grow up believing that the Bible was no more than "a collection of myths," undermining the nation's Christian faith and replacing a religion of love and peace with the doctrine of survival of the fittest.

Bryan's fear of social Darwinism was not entirely unfounded. Evolutionary thinking had helped to give birth to the eugenics movement, which maintained that one could breed a better person in the same way that farmers bred better sheep and cattle. Eugenics led to now-discredited theories of race and class superiority that helped drive the debate over immigration in the US and led some American states to enact sterilization laws to stop "mental deficients" from having children.

Most who favored the teaching of evolution in public schools were not supporters of eugenics but simply wanted students to be exposed to the most up-to-date scientific thinking. For others, like supporters of the newly formed American Civil Liberties Union, teaching evolution was an issue of freedom of speech as well as a matter of maintaining the separation of church and state. Still others, like famed lawyer Clarence Darrow, saw the battle over evolution as a proxy for a wider cultural conflict between what they considered progress and modernity, on the one side, and what they viewed as religious superstition and backwardness, on the other. Darrow, for one, believed that religion, particularly Christianity, led to unnecessary division within society and was an enemy of social progress.

Scopes and Its Aftermath

At the urging of Bryan and evangelical Christian leaders, evolution opponents tried to ban the teaching of Darwin's theory in a number of states, including Kentucky and Florida. Although these efforts failed, evolution opponents eventually won a victory in 1925 when the Tennessee Legislature overwhelmingly approved legislation making it a crime to teach "any theory that denies the story of the Divine Creation of man as taught in the Bible, and to teach instead that man has descended from a lower order of animal." Soon after the Tennessee law was enacted, the ACLU offered to defend any science teacher in the state who was willing to break it. John Scopes, a teacher in the small, rural town of Dayton, Tenn., agreed to take up the ACLU's offer.

Meanwhile, Bryan and Darrow agreed to assist the prosecution and defense, respectively – turning an already highly publicized event into a media circus. Indeed, *State of Tennessee v. Scopes* (1925), popularly referred to as the *Scopes* "monkey" trial, was one of the first true media trials of the modern era, covered in hundreds of newspapers and broadcast live on radio. From the start, both sides seemed to agree that the case was being tried more in the court of public opinion than in a court of law.

Darrow and the ACLU legal team focused their attacks on the Tennessee statute, which they cited as a violation of church-state separation, and on the notion that biblical revelation could be an adequate substitute for science in the classroom. But state prosecutors effectively blocked the defense team's efforts in this regard, arguing that the issue before the court was not the Bible nor even the statute, but whether Scopes had violated the law.

As the trial progressed, it seemed increasingly clear that the defense team's hope of turning the case into a public debate about the merits of teaching evolution was being stymied by state prosecutors. But just when it seemed that the *Scopes* case might end with a whimper, Darrow made the highly unorthodox request of calling Bryan to the witness stand. Although the politician was under no obligation to testify, he acceded to Darrow's invitation.

With Bryan on the stand, Darrow proceeded to ask a series of detailed questions about biblical events that could be seen as inconsistent, unreal or both. For instance, Darrow asked, how could there be morning and evening during the first three days of biblical creation if the sun was not formed until the fourth? And was Jonah really swallowed by a whale? Bryan responded to these and similar questions in different ways. Often, he defended the biblical account in question as the literal truth, the work of a God of miracles. On other occasions, however, he admitted that something in Scripture might need to be interpreted in order to be fully accepted.

Although the largely local crowd observing the two-hour exchange was clearly on Bryan's side, most journalists and other observers believed that Darrow's cross-examination made his opponent seem inconsistent, flustered and, at times, even buffoonish. The next day, many big city papers hailed Darrow and savaged Bryan, who unexpectedly died less than a week later. And while Scopes was convicted of violating the anti-evolution law and fined, his conviction was later overturned on a technicality by the Tennessee Supreme Court.

Meanwhile, the trial, particularly Darrow's questioning of Bryan, created a tremendous amount of positive publicity for the pro-evolution camp, especially in northern urban areas, where the media and cultural elites were sympathetic toward Scopes and his defense. But this post-*Scopes* momentum did not destroy the anti-evolution movement. Indeed, in the years immediately following *Scopes*, two additional state legislatures – in Mississippi and Arkansas – enacted bills similar to the Tennessee law. Other states, particularly in the South and Midwest, passed resolutions condemning the inclusion of material on evolution in biology textbooks. These actions, along with a patchwork of restrictions from local school boards, prompted most publishers to remove references to Darwin from their science textbooks.

Efforts to make evolution the standard in all biology classes would have to wait a number of decades before bearing any fruit. This was due in large part to the fact that the government prohibition on religious establishment or favoritism, found in the Establishment Clause in the First Amendment to the US Constitution, applied only to federal and not state actions. This meant that state governments were free to set their own policies on church-state issues. Only in 1947, with the Supreme Court's decision in *Everson v. Board of Education*, did the constitutional prohibition on religious establishment begin to apply to state as well as federal actions. Efforts to mandate the teaching of evolution also received a boost 10 years after *Everson*, in 1957, when the surprise Soviet launch of the first satellite, Sputnik I, prompted the United States to make science education a national priority.

Epperson and Edwards: The Supreme Court Intervenes

In 1968, in *Epperson v. Arkansas*, the Supreme Court finally turned its attention to anti-evolution laws. The case concerned a challenge to a 1928 post-*Scopes* Arkansas law that made it a crime to teach evolution in a public school or state university. The law did not require the teaching of creationism or any other theory of life's origins and development but simply barred Darwinian evolution from the state's public educational system.

In a 9-0 decision, the high court ruled that the Arkansas law violated the First Amendment's Establishment Clause because it ultimately had a religious purpose, in this case preventing students from learning a particular viewpoint antithetical to theologically conservative Christianity. "There can be no doubt that Arkansas has sought to prevent its teachers from discussing the theory of evolution because it is contrary to the belief of some that the Book of Genesis must be the exclusive source of doctrine as to the origin of man," Justice Abe Fortas wrote for the majority. Using state power to advance this end, Fortas concluded, clearly amounted to an establishment of religion and hence was contrary to the First Amendment's Establishment Clause.

Epperson put an end to state and local prohibitions on teaching evolution. Even before the case had been decided, however, a new anti-evolution movement, dubbed "creation science" or "scientific creationism," was taking shape and beginning to influence the wider debate. Proponents of creation science contend that the weight of scientific evidence supports the creation story described in the biblical book of Genesis – with the formation of the earth and the development of life occurring in six 24-hour days. The presence of fossils and evidence of significant geological change are attributed to the great catastrophic flood described in the eighth chapter of Genesis, in which all life on Earth's surface was destroyed save Noah, his family and the animals they had taken with them in the ark.

Throughout the late 19th and early 20th centuries, many conservative Christians had come to believe that the Earth was much older than the approximately 6,000 years biblical scholars had long estimated it to be. A turn toward what is known as "young Earth creationism" can be traced to 1961, when engineer Henry M. Morris and theologian John C. Whitcomb published *The*

Genesis Flood. The book became the bible of the creation science movement, purporting to present scientific explanations for the creation, destruction and repopulation of the Earth as described in the book of Genesis.

The Genesis Flood became and remains a bestseller, helping to spawn a network of creation science think tanks, including the Institute for Creation Research, founded by Morris in 1970. Furthermore, in the wake of the *Epperson* ruling, creation science provided an alternative to the now-unconstitutional efforts to ban the teaching of evolution in public schools. In the early 1980s, two states, Arkansas and Louisiana, embraced creation science, passing what their legislatures called "balanced treatment" statutes that required creation science to be taught alongside evolution.

Both statutes were ultimately the subject of legal challenges. In 1982, the Arkansas law was struck down by a federal district court in *McLean v. Arkansas Board of Education*. In its analysis of the statute, the district court relied on a 1971 Supreme Court decision, *Lemon v. Kurtzman*, which set up a three-part test to determine whether a government action violates the Establishment Clause. Under the "*Lemon* test," an action must have a bona fide secular purpose, must not advance or inhibit religion and must not excessively entangle the government with religion. If the challenged action fails any one of the three parts of the *Lemon* test, it is deemed to have violated the Establishment Clause.

In *McLean*, District Judge William Overton ruled that the Arkansas law violated the Establishment Clause because it did not satisfy any of the *Lemon* test's three prongs. Overton noted that both the author of the act and those who lobbied for it publicly acknowledged its sectarian purpose, which, he said, was otherwise clear from an objective reading of it. Furthermore, Overton determined that creation science was not science, but based wholly on the biblical creation story. Therefore, he wrote, the teaching of creation science clearly advanced religion and entangled it with the government.

The US Supreme Court entered the creation science debate five years later in *Edwards v. Aguillard* (1987), a case that, like *McLean*, involved a challenge to a balanced treatment law, this one from Louisiana. Like the Arkansas statute, the Louisiana act forbade the teaching of the theory of evolution in public schools unless it was accompanied by instruction in creation science. In a 7-2 decision, the Supreme Court ruled that the act violated the Establishment Clause because it did not meet the first, or secular-purpose, prong of the *Lemon* test. The high court did not bother to consider the second and third prongs of the test, since failure to satisfy any of the three is sufficient to nullify a government action.

Writing for the majority, Justice William Brennan stated that "the pre-eminent purpose of the Louisiana Legislature was clearly to advance the religious viewpoint that a supernatural being created humankind." He dismissed the state's contention that the aim of the act was to protect academic freedom and make the teaching of science more comprehensive. Actually, Brennan argued, the Louisiana law severely limited both aims by prohibiting the teaching of evolution unless certain other conditions were met. Furthermore, he maintained, the act's legislative history clearly showed that the statute's primary sponsor in the Louisiana Legislature hoped that passage would lead to the teaching of neither evolution nor creation science. If academic freedom and comprehensiveness were actually the purpose of the act, Brennan wrote, "it would have encouraged the teaching of all scientific theories about the origins of mankind." Finally, Brennan left open the door for schools to teach other scientifically based critiques of evolution. "Teaching a variety of scientific theories about the origins of humankind to schoolchildren might be validly done with the clear secular intent of enhancing the effectiveness of science instruction," he wrote.

Justice Antonin Scalia, in a dissenting opinion joined by Chief Justice William Rehnquist, took the majority to task for presuming to divine the actual, as opposed to the stated, intentions of the Louisiana Legislature. Scalia pointed out that the legislators had sworn an oath to uphold the Constitution, understood the potential Establishment Clause problems and had taken several months to craft a bill that tried to meet these concerns. Given these facts, he wrote, the majority was essentially saying "that the members of the Louisiana Legislature knowingly violated their oaths and then lied about it."

Scalia also criticized the majority for presuming to determine whether creation science was actually science and worth teaching in schools. Such a determination was the responsibility of the Louisiana Legislature, not federal courts, he said. Even if the legislators were wrong, Scalia argued, their error should not be deemed unconstitutional, as long as they sincerely believed that creation science was actually science.

The Battle Over Disclaimers

Neither *Edwards* nor *Epperson* prohibits the teaching of biblical creationism in other contexts, such as part of a literature or world religions class. The Supreme Court has made clear in a number of cases involving the role of religion in schools that "the Bible may constitutionally be used in an appropriate study of history, civilization, ethics, comparative religion or the like" (*Stone v. Graham*, 1980). Nevertheless, *Edwards* essentially ended state efforts to bring creation science into public school science classes. As already noted, recent anti-evolution efforts have focused on other strategies, such as disclaimers and, in the last decade, intelligent design.

Efforts to require either oral or written evolution disclaimers have not met with success in federal courts. In a 1999 decision, *Freiler v. Tangipahoa Parish (La.) Board of Education*, the 5th US Circuit Court of Appeals invalidated a disclaimer that teachers were expected to read to students in Tangipahoa, La., before beginning instruction in evolution. The statement in question urged students learning about evolution "to exercise critical thinking and gather all information possible and closely examine each alternative toward forming an opinion." It also stated that teaching evolution was "not intended to influence or dissuade the biblical version of Creation or any other concept." Writing for a unanimous three-judge panel,

The Social and Legal Dimensions of the US Evolution Debate

Judge Fortunato "Pete" Benavides determined that the disclaimer violated the second or "effect" prong of the *Lemon* test (which prohibits actions that advance or inhibit religion), concluding that "the primary effect of the disclaimer is to protect and maintain a particular religious viewpoint, namely belief in the biblical version of Creation."

The most recent disclaimer case, *Selman v. Cobb County School District* (2005), also fell afoul of the *Lemon* test's second prong. Unlike the oral disclaimer in *Freiler*, the statement approved by the Cobb County, Ga., school board was to be affixed to textbooks and did not mention the Bible, the biblical creation story or even religion. It read: "This textbook contains material on evolution. Evolution is a theory, not a fact, regarding the origin of living things. This material should be approached with an open mind, studied carefully and critically considered."

In *Selman*, District Judge Clarence Cooper ruled that while the disclaimer had a legitimate secular purpose (in this case, "fostering critical thinking"), it had the effect of advancing religion, due to the historical context in which most people in the area would view it. Indeed, Cooper wrote, because of longstanding opposition to teaching Darwin's theory by many evangelical Christians and others in Cobb County, "the sticker sends a message to those who oppose evolution for religious reasons that they are favored members of the political community, while the sticker sends a message to those who believe in evolution that they are political outsiders."

A New Challenge: Intelligent Design

Most recently, courts have grappled with a new challenge to Darwinian evolution: intelligent design. Advocates of intelligent design argue that living systems are so complex that they could not have evolved purely by evolution through natural selection and instead must have been directed or designed by an outside force, most likely God. In particular, supporters of intelligent design point to what they say are "irreducibly complex" systems, such as the eye or the process by which blood clots, as proof that Darwinian evolution is not an adequate explanation for the development of life.

The great majority of scientists reject intelligent design, claiming that it is little more than creationism dressed up in scientific jargon. Many scientists do not even want to debate intelligent design proponents, arguing that doing so would give the movement a legitimacy it does not deserve.

Still, a small but highly visible cadre of researchers and thinkers contend that intelligent design will soon become a full-fledged, legitimate scientific theory. The modern intelligent design movement is only roughly two decades old, they point out. Indeed, the issue did not receive widespread attention until 1991, when Phillip Johnson, a law professor at the University of California at Berkeley, published his first book on the subject, *Darwin on Trial*. Even some proponents of intelligent design hesitate to treat the idea as a full-fledged theory; for instance, the nation's premiere intelligent design think tank, the Discovery Institute in Seattle, opposed efforts to insert any mention of intelligent design into a high school biology curriculum, arguing that the theory is not developed enough to be taught in high schools.

But in October 2004, the school board in Dover, Penn., voted to include a brief mention of intelligent design in its high school biology curriculum. The resolution required teachers to read a lengthy disclaimer before students began learning about Darwinian evolution. The disclaimer stated, in part, that evolution was a "theory," that "gaps in the theory exist for which there is no evidence" and that "Intelligent Design is an explanation of the origin of life that differs from Darwin's view." A number of area families with children in the public school system then sued the board in federal district court, claiming that the new policy was unconstitutional.

In *Kitzmiller v. Dover Area School District* (2005) the district court struck down the new requirement, determining that it was an unconstitutional endorsement of religion. In his lengthy decision, District Judge John E. Jones III ruled that intelligent design is not science but "a religious argument" and "nothing less than the progeny of creationism." Jones noted that in *Edwards*, the Supreme Court made it unconstitutional for public schools to teach creation science. More specifically, the judge ruled that because the school board singled out evolution for a disclaimer and introduced a religion-friendly alternative, "an objective student would view the disclaimer as a strong official endorsement of religion." Moreover, Jones ruled, the actions of the school board clearly showed that they were motivated by a desire to "advance religion," thus violating the first prong of the *Lemon* test.

The *Kitzmiller* decision was not appealed. All but one of the school board members who endorsed the curriculum change were not re-elected in November 2005, a month before the court decision. Their replacements did not support the teaching of intelligent design and had no interest in continuing to fight for a policy they fundamentally opposed.

Federal courts again weighed in on the question of evolution and science curricula five years later in *Association of Christian Schools International et al. v. Roman Stearns et al.* Calvary Chapel Christian School – an evangelical Protestant school – and a number of its students sued the University of California system after university officials determined that a number of science courses taught at Calvary Chapel did not meet the university's admissions standards because they gave little or no attention to evolution. A federal district court in California ruled that the university system's policy was not unconstitutional, and that decision was upheld by the 9th US Circuit Court of Appeals. The Supreme Court declined to review the case, meaning the 9th Circuit ruling stands.

Battles over teaching evolution in schools did not end with the *Association of Christian Schools International* ruling. In 2013 alone, challenges to teaching evolution sprung up in school boards and legislatures in roughly a dozen states, making it likely that courts will once again be called upon to rule on some aspect of the controversy.

10

Catholicism and Politics in the Modern Era
The Pontifical Academy of Social Sciences

The Pontifical Academy of Social Sciences was established by Pope John Paul II in 1994 with the aim of promoting the study and progress of the social sciences, thus offering the Catholic Church those elements which can be used in the development of social doctrine.

This viewpoint looks at the ways in which the Catholic Church has responded to contemporary social issues and events in the twentieth and twenty-first centuries. Since the Second Vatican Council (Vatican II, 1962-1965), the Church has made an effort to react to social issues around the world, showing a greater engagement with the secular world than had previously been the case. Through looking at how the Church views its role in society, we can better understand the role of Catholicism in political and social issues today.

The assigned topic of this paper is to analyze how the Catholic Church has engaged the modern world, particularly in the twentieth century. The assignment offered license to advance into this century and I will take advantage of that invitation. Both terms, Church and world, admit of expansive definitions. For this paper the teaching of the Second Vatican Council will provide the understanding for both terms. Hence the Church, understood as both a community of disciples, "The People of God", and the social institution which structures the community are used as the

---

"How Catholic Social Teaching Engages the World Situation," the Pontifical Academy of Social Sciences, http://www.pass.va/content/scienzesociali/en/events/2014-18/centesimus_annus/hehir.html. Licensed under CC BY-SA 4.0.

dogmatic constitution on the Church, "Lumen Gentium" describes them. The world for the purposes of this paper can be understood as the pastoral constitution of the council, "Gaudium et Spes" describes it:

> Therefore, the world which the Council has in mind is the whole human family seen in the context of everything which envelopes it: it is the world as the theatre of human history, bearing the marks of its travail, its triumphs and its failures, the world which in the Christian vision has been created and is sustained by the love of its maker which has been freed from the slavery of sin by Christ.

While this theological description of the world will have to be joined to a more empirical description in this paper, the basic theme of "Gaudium et Spes" is that the Church is always in the world, surrounded, challenged and questioned by its complexity. The Church has engaged the world since time of the New Testament. Such engagement has involved its hierarchical leadership and the community it leads.

[…]

From Conciliar to Papal Engagement: Two Examples

In the historiography of twentieth century Catholicism a tripartite framework is widely used: pre-conciliar, conciliar and post-conciliar experience of the Catholic community and its hierarchical institutions. The consensual judgement about Vatican II is that it purposefully opened a new style of engagement between the Church and the world. "Gaudium et Spes" is taken as the premier example of the engagement. Beyond that consensus there is a lively debate about the consequences of the engagement begun at the Council. While words and deeds of the papacy do not exhaust Catholic life, particularly since the Council, they do hold a unique role, influence and significance. Here I focus on the style and substance of the engagement of John Paul II (1978-2005) and Francis (2013-).

Pope John Paul II: The Pope as (Prophetic) Statesman

In both the life of the Catholic Church and the life of the world, Karol Wojtyla was a person who embodied the history of the last century. As a citizen of Poland, he and his family were impacted by the three wars of the century: born just after World War I, he lived through the fatal European consequences of the 1930s, then he prepared for the priesthood secretly during the Nazi occupation and World War II; finally, he became a major part of the history of the Cold War. Simultaneously, his life spanned the theological and ecclesial preparation for Vatican II; he had deep engagement in the Council itself and he exercised major episcopal leadership in Poland until he was elected to the Chair of Peter. This range of experiences involved the Church and world. In light of them, but without description of them, this assessment will be confined to his papacy. He brought with him, to the office of the papacy, his experiences as a priest, a philosopher and a bishop. He lived under an atheistic regime in a profoundly Catholic country, and he lived in a centralized command economy which existed along with a vibrant intellectual culture tied to the history of Poland.

Internally, in the life of the church his pontificate is known for his enormous magisterial output, for his global pastoral travel and for his centralization of authority in Rome even though he spoke regularly, and with conviction, about the meaning of collegiality as a style of leadership. A topic which continually is discussed was his participation in Vatican II and then his assessment of the dynamics of post-conciliar Catholicism. Regarding his commitment to the teaching of Vatican II, George Weigel, in his massive biography of John Paul II, is surely accurate when he says: "That John Paul II understands himself to be a man of the Second Vatican Council is indisputable on the public record."[17] Starting with this baseline, it is still legitimate to ask about the Pope's convictions about the post-conciliar era. Both Paul VI and John Paul II were openly critical of how the Council and post-conciliar dynamic was interpreted by some laity and clergy, by some theologians and historians. In John Paul II's case, faced with more pluralism that he thought tolerable, he moved to reshape the dynamic and the discussion by focusing on three key loci in the church: appointment of bishops, the writings of theologians and the life of religious communities. In all three instances the internal policy of the Pope can fairly be described as determination to direct the consequences of the Council in ways which often met with respectful but real resistance, yet also found sustained support over twenty-seven years.

While John Paul II's leadership within the Church requires extensive analysis to be adequate, the theme of "engagement with the world situation" is primarily about his leadership on the wider world stage in pursuit of justice, peace and human rights. The world situation he encountered is best understood as two phases of his long papacy. Phase I (1978-1990) included his election as pope and extended to the collapse of the communist empire, first in Central Eastern Europe and then within the Soviet Union as a whole. During these years "the world situation" was quite similar to the world which confronted the Vatican Council. Until the communist demise, the world of bipolarity, severe nuclear danger and superpower competition were the visible characteristics of world politics. The continuing process of decolonization and the challenges facing newly independent states were a distinct narrative, as was continuing conflicts within the Middle East. Phase II (1990-2005) brought deep and powerful changes in the world, which John Paul II addressed in "Centesimus Annus". Bipolarity collapsed but there was little scholarly agreement about what configuration of states would replace it. Indeed, the events of 2001 (the 9-11 attacks) illustrated that world politics was no longer just about states. Transnational actors, of very different kinds and with different goals, had been expanding since the 1960's; but transnational terror of the 9/11 kind brought very new challenges. The tripartite division of the world which analysts used for three decades no longer yielded either clarity or accuracy in analyzing the world. The interdependence of the 1970s had developed into the distinct phenomenon of globalization with all its diverse consequences: economic, political, and moral.

John Paul II, from the moment of his election, brought to this world – in both its phases – a unique range of experience and talents. A pope who was a philosopher and an actor, an intellectual and an athlete, a pastor whose priesthood and episcopacy had been honed in conflict with an atheistic state and a centralized command economy. Beyond these characteristics, however, the critical factor for understanding his sense of engagement was a capacious conception of pastoral and public leadership. This conception of the papacy would be evident in what he said and did for over a quarter of a century. His sense of history and his understanding of the Church's relationship to historical change permeated his writing and preaching and shaped the choices he made. It can be traced from his first address to the United Nations (1979) through the writing of "Centesimus Annus" (especially his reflection on "The Year 1989") and on to his focus on leading the church "across the threshold" into a new century.

Beyond this broadly defined, activist conception of leadership, John Paul II added another dimension, leadership which was global in scope. The office of the papacy, of course, is universal by nature. He made a universal office global through 104 trips crisscrossing the world in every year of his papacy. When he died, a standard part of the commentary about him was that he likely had been seen in person by more people than any other historical figure. Leadership which was activist and global, two dimensions of engagement. The engagement, however, was carefully structured; he consistently defined his trips as pastoral visits to the local churches. Yet he traveled as a head of state, so the visits were never without their secular implications. At times he would defend the local church from pressure or harassment (Poland – the unique example); at other times he would press the church hierarchy to take a stronger stance on human rights (Haiti, an example); at other times his goal was to open doors long closed to the church (Cuba).

Since the trips were pastoral, John Paul never shied away from explicit religious language with papal Masses always being major events. But when he engaged governments, the principal means of engagement was the language and logic of human rights. The appeal was not for favoritism or privilege for his church, but an argument of reason supporting the rights of each and all.

In his two addresses to the United Nations, a setting at once secular and universal, the philosopher-pope was at work. In 1979 he praised the United Nations for its Declaration on Human rights (1948) and then dove into one of the continuing disputes at the institution and beyond it: how to define and relate political-civil rights to socio-economic rights. He fashioned his own analysis, framing the debate in terms of spiritual and material goods, arguing for both but carefully giving priority to the former. In secular and religious settings, he would make the case that the right to religious freedom was the fundamental human right after life itself. For a Church which had made an explicit case for this right only at Vatican II (1965), this claim could be a source of surprise to many, but no one doubted the Pope's commitment to the full range of basic rights.

In addition to this global, activist, rights-based ministry of engagement a final characteristic was John Paul II's willingness, indeed eagerness, to engage multiple forums where the church's relationship to the world could be described, analyzed and engaged by others in dialogue. In addition to the U.N. General Assembly, the International Labor Organization and the multiple meetings with heads of state and other diplomats, John Paul II carried on his own personal work of the "New Evangelization" in the Vatican, in Rome and beyond.

His method of engagement can be examined, but not exhaustively, in terms of three substantive dimensions of it.

First, his style of engagement flowed directly from "Gaudium et Spes". He had been part of the drafting and revision of this text during the Council, and he located his engagement directly and solidly in the defense of the human person. In his first encyclical, "Redemptor Hominis" (1979) he stated that the human person is: "the primary and fundamental way for the Church..." (#14) The sentence set the direction for his ministry of engagement. It corresponds to the assertion in "Gaudium et Spes" that the Church "is at once the sign and the safeguard of the transcendental dimension of the human person" (#76). As noted above locating the social ministry of the church in the defense of the human person was not new, but John Paul II also followed the deeper, broader definition of this connection which is found in the conciliar text. Over twenty years after "Redemptor Hominis", John Paul II returns to the theme in "Centesimus Annus":

> We are not dealing here with man in the "abstract", but with the real "concrete", "historical" man. We are dealing with each individual, since each one is included in the mystery of Redemption and through this mystery Christ has united himself with each one forever. It follows the Church cannot abandon man and that this man is the primary route that the Church must travel in fulfilling her mission. (#53)

These statements provide two resources for a ministry of engagement. First, the person is the criterion by which the church at every level and in every place decides which issues to pursue in the public arena. Second, this linkage of the person and the church provides a secular rationale to explain and defend the church's public role. The church is in the public arena to defend human dignity and support human rights.

Second, the Pope's engagement with the world included significant attention in word and deed to the role and place of the state in relation to the church and society. At the outset it should be said that anyone who writes on John Paul II's views on the state should attend carefully to Professor Russell Hittinger's analysis of the theme in the Fordham International Law Jounral. Hittinger advances a very precise proposition: "The chief thesis of this article is that "Centesimus Annus" makes a decisive turn toward the liberal model of the state." He makes clear that he is not saying that the Pope's view of the state is dependent on either eighteenth century democratic models or liberal philosophies of the West. I find persuasive Hittinger's argument that John Paul II has advanced Catholic understanding of the role of the state in society and its relationship to the church. As part of his argument, based on a close reading of "Centesimus Annus," he makes a case regarding Pope John Paul's suspicion of the state itself and how he seeks to contain and restrain it. Containing the power of the state is a basic idea of liberalism, but from the perspective of how the Pope engages states in his ministry I find it difficult to verify the deep suspicion of the state as such that is part of Professor Hittinger's analysis.

Admittedly, I am focusing upon the level of practical engagement with the state, which is not the principal concern of Hittinger's article. From the perspective of engagement, I find John Paul II's style to be Gelasian and Conciliar, that is a mix of Pope Gelasius (496) and Vatican II. The Gelasian tradition advocates in principle mutual respect of church and state, recognition by both parties of the legitimacy of the other, and a conviction that their roles are complementary. It also implies, to be sure, recognition that resistance at times is necessary to protect the legitimate interests of each party. Indeed, invoking John Courtney Murray again, he draws a line from Gelasius in the fifth century to Pope Gregory VII (1073-1085) in the eleventh century and celebrates Gregory's strong support of freedom of the church in the face of state intrusion. To be sure, John Paul II invoked this restraint often. His ministry in Poland required constant vigilance.

The Hittinger article is not cast as a church-state argument; it is more about the state's role in society, a topic which runs through papal social teaching and forms part of John Paul II's social encyclicals. I agree that "Centesimus Annus" endorses strong restraints on the state, invoking both the principle of subsidiarity and the role of human rights.

Here again, Murray's work and Hittinger's are at least analogous but not identical (in part because Murray died in 1967). The Hittinger article, stressing the liberal state model as a new development in the Catholic corpus of social teaching, seems to me to omit Murray's argument that the move away from Leo XIII's broad conception of "the ethical state", with an expansive moral role for the state, had been progressively pursued, beginning with Pius XII then leading on to "Pacem In Terris" (1963) and finding adoption in Vatican II's "Dignitatis Humanae". Murray describes the process as the move from "the ethical state" to "the juridical" model of the state. My point is not to focus on different wording, but rather to see "Centesimus Annus" as located within this larger process of development. It is also what is meant by the conciliar approach of John Paul II to the role of the state as found in "Dignitatis Humanae". If accurate, this may yield a less suspicious attitude toward the state than Hittinger finds in "Centesimus Annus". I stress I am trying to identify how John Paul II engaged the state in practice. The Gelasian-Conciliar model provides for restraint on the state in sacral and in societal matters, but it also yields a recognition of the state's unique role in human affairs, domestically and internationally. Moreover, such a view, in principle, seeks structured collaboration with the state in pursuit of the common good.

While the state-society relationship provoked some attention after the publication of "Centesimus Annus", the more prominent debate concerned the state-market relationship. The issue here was whether the liberal turn, which Professor Hittinger and others identified in the encyclical, was meant to recast papal teaching on the role of the state in the economic sector. The stress in "Centesimus Annus" on the potential of the business or market economy, the emphasis given to the need to foster innovation and freedom in the economic arena, both raised questions of whether the intent of the encyclical (after the collapse of communism) was simply to endorse a very liberal state; some strong advocates argued this case of greater market freedom. The text of "Centesimus Annus" provided some grounds for this debate.

It should be noted that John Paul II did not initiate a new theme with this encyclical. The appropriate role of the state in the socio-economic order has run through the social teaching since

Leo XIII. John XXIII provided impetus to analysis in his discussion of the relationship between the principle of subsidiarity and the fact of socialization, preserving the principle of subsidiarity but adapting it to new needs.

To be sure Pope John Paul II has provided a welcome degree of specificity in his analysis of the market economy. Previous Catholic teaching had often tried to provide a via media between the premises of a market economy and a more expansive role for the state arising from social welfare states in Europe. The role of the market was acknowledged but usually provided modest normative support.

John Paul II in "Centesimus Annus" establishes a new framework. First, he identifies the positive potential of the role of the market; used effectively and with balance it contributes to a rational allocation of resources, it promotes initiative and innovation and it can be a protection for the citizen against the reach of the state. Second, the Pope himself offers a balancing argument, namely, the market by itself will not secure justice in the economy. In the words of the encyclical: "Here we find a new limit on the market: there are collective and quantitative needs which cannot be satisfied by market mechanisms. There are important human needs which escape its logic. There are goods which by their very nature cannot and must not be bought or sold." (#49)

It is because of these limitations, inherent in the dynamic of the market economy, that John Paul II argues that a juridical framework should be established within which the assets of the market can function, but basic human needs will be met. The language recalls Murray's definition of the "juridical state".

To return to the discussion of the liberal state, it is clear that "Centesimus Annus" does place clear limits on the state, as well as the market, but in the broader range of Pope John Paul's social teaching, the state also has positive social functions. Here again, John Paul II has his own way of describing these functions. In paragraph fifteen he refers to the state-market relationship by affirming that the state "has the task of determining the juridical

The Role of Religion in Public Policy

framework within which economic affairs are to be conducted." He then distinguishes two roles for the state: an "indirect role" of creating favorable conditions for economic activity, and a "direct role" of defending the weakest and ensuring the necessary minimum support for the unemployed. This specification of the direct role establishes a principle, but a more detailed analysis of it would have to ask whether the direct role includes a guarantee of a "social safety net" which Catholic social teaching seems to imply. Here "Mater et Magistra" (1961) and "Pacen In Terris" (1963) would provide points of reference.

Third, John Paul II's engagement went beyond specific society-state relations; he engaged "the world" in two broader senses. There was the world of the international relations, what was commonly called the international system; and there was the world as "Gaudium et Spes" had described the complex, multidimensional reality which is the setting for the church's ministry. Some commentary is needed about Pope John Paul's engagement with both meanings of the world.

As noted above, his pontificate began in the depths of the Cold War, but the greater part of his ministry was exercised in the post-cold war era. In secular commentary, he is usually identified with his role in bringing the Cold War to an end. There is no question about the critical significance of how this "Pope from the Second World" exercised his religious ministry from 1978-1990 in a fashion which gave it unique political significance. No less an authority than Michael Gorbachev has testified to the centrality of John Paul II's influence. Ten years after the collapse of communism, Gorbachev said: "What has happened in Eastern Europe in recent years would not have been possible without the presence of this pope."[27]

But this dimension of his engagement, the role he played in the East-West conflict, should not be seen as his exclusive concern or sole focus. The Cold War had both an East-West and a North-South dimension. In both his travels and his teaching John Paul II was a constant advocate for reshaping world politics to meet the needs of "the global South". In "Sollicitudo Rei Socialis" he criticized the dynamic of "the logic of the blocs", his way of describing how the East-West conflict directly harmed the South. In "Centesimus Annus" he returned to the theme, quite explicitly placing his advocacy for the South just after his argument that the nations of Central and Eastern Europe would require major assistance after the collapse of communism.

John Paul II's travels matched his advocacy; he made repeated trips to Latin America and Africa over a twenty-five-year papacy. These trips often had a dual purpose: to support the local church which often ministered in the midst of conflict and poverty, and to be a voice for the global South both during and after the Cold War.

Beyond his direct engagement with international politics – always in a religious sense, usually invoking the theme of human rights as his chosen mode of advocacy, John Paul carried forward the dialogue which "Gaudium et Spes" initiated and invited the church to pursue with the world. In this dialogue, "the world" was never purely states or world politics. It was a much broader intellectual, cultural and economic reality. "Gaudium et Spes" purposely intended to engage the world in style and substance differently than the previous century had characterized the church's role. Karl Rahner described this dimension of church-world engagement:

> *The Council has opened up a dialogue with the world. It actually did not and, of course, could not itself carry out this dialogue. But during its sessions the Council clearly began to see the world of the modern mind, that is, the world of a pluralistic, scientific, technically oriented society of vast scope and multiplicity of insights and tendencies, a world of a contested and divided Christianity, one of the world religions, a world with an immense future waiting to be planned.*

Rahner's description of "the world" fit well the post-industrial democracies of Western Europe, North America and Japan. It was not an adequate description for much of the global South. While John Paul, from his trips and his constant engagement with bishops throughout the world, knew well it was a partial world Rahner described, he also recognized its importance, for it would influence "the world" eventually beyond the borders of Europe and North America. On that basis he sought to engage the partial version of "the world" in terms of how its cultures, its universities and its media were fashioning an understanding of the meaning of life, of the role of religion and the modern world order. The Pope's engagement with the world Rahner described cut across a broad range of issues: from bioethics to economics, from culture to politics, and from philosophy to faith, he was determined that the church's vision of life, its voice for human rights and its conception of moral solidarity would not be absent in the globalizing world he saw emerging. But John Paul II never ceased to remind Rahner's world of its responsibilities and its limits. There were other dialogues for the church in the global south and he never omitted them in his engagement with the world. The issues engaged the social ministry of the church, but also the role local churches could play in the life of their societies.

He fashioned a global ministry in multiple forums: the pulpit, the lectern, the United Nations and the world of states all heard and saw repeatedly his witness.

Pope Francis: A Prophetic Papacy

Pope Francis's engagement with the world has been recorded, televised, tweeted and celebrated across national, religious and global lines. In a brief pontificate thus far, he has brought together inside and beyond the Church, a unique assembly of supporters and collaborators. His capacity for engagement across secular and sacral lines is never in doubt.

The "world situation" he has encountered is, to a great degree, an extension of the world which both John Paul II and Benedict XVI addressed as pastors and teachers. Politically, it is less well defined than the Cold War configuration; economically, it is a world still in recovery, at different levels, from the financial crisis of 2007-09. While the danger of major nuclear war has declined, the possibility of the use of nuclear weapons remains; war in this world is primarily the kind of brutal internal conflict which joins civil war with outside intervention by states and transnational terrorism. Religiously, at least in the southern hemisphere, the secularization thesis has been contradicted to a great degree.

Pope Francis, of course, is both non-European and a citizen from the global South. As John Paul II's Polish and European background shaped his papacy, so Pope Francis brings with him key characteristics which are reflected in his ministry. These include his background as a Jesuit, his experience as a Latin American bishop during the fifty tumultuous and creative years for the Church in Latin America since Vatican II, and his commitment to the vision of that Council. These characteristics are dimensions of how he addresses global and national economies, the relationship of the environment and the poor and the concrete awareness he has of the costs of internal conflicts within states.

The first characteristic of his engagement with the Church and the world is his own persona. From the day of his election and address to the crowds in St. Peter's square to the present, very concrete details of his life – where he lives, what car carries him, what vestments he chooses have all been of global interest. To a multi-religious and a secular world his person communicates humility and holiness. But neither characteristic has limited his conviction that the office of the papacy must play a vocal demonstrative role at this time in history. While he has addressed a wide range of daily issues in his homilies and audiences, in his major teaching documents three macro-issues of global and national significance stand out; poverty and inequality; immigration; and the environment. These topics, which cut vertically through the world from global to national to local levels of human life, have provided him with the opportunity of speaking from his deepest convictions about the theme of "the globalization of indifference".

Those convictions have found expression in two different documents: "Evangelii Gaudium" and "Laudato Si". This first is an apostolic exhortation to the Church; the second is the encyclical directed to the Church and the world. While they are formally different in authority, that distinction is far less important than the substantive themes which tie the texts together. Both are classical calls to engagement; "Evangelii Gaudium" calls Christians to renew their encounter with Christ and to be agents of evangelization in the world; "Laudato Si" speaks from within the Church but calls Church and world to the engagement of care for the world we share. In both documents the poor of the world are a connecting theme. Engagement for Pope Francis is being a voice against "an economy of exclusion" and an advocate for addressing inequality. In "Laudato Si," Pope Francis draws widespread admiration for providing the moral framework which can identify the global challenge of climate change and join it again and again with the fate of the world and the fate of the poor.

In addressing these and other threats to human dignity, Pope Francis uses a combination of words and deeds. This is a second characteristic of his style of engagement. To some degree it is reflective of John Paul II combining his background as a teacher and an actor. Pope Francis joins his passionate address to the world about immigration with his visits to Lampedusa and the Jesuit refugee center in Rome. He combines his abiding references to poverty and exclusion with opening showers in the Vatican for the homeless in Rome and visits to soup kitchens and prisons on his visits abroad. His call for lifestyle changes as part of the response to the environmental crisis is combined with his own austerity and frugality.

A third characteristic involves his commitment to Vatican II's teaching on collegiality. Pope Francis clearly has a sense of urgency about leading the Church to address the dominant issues of our time, but he wants to lead not as a solo performance but in cooperation with the worldwide episcopal college. This is an evident mark of his style of engagement in two senses. First, he calls the leaders of local churches to take the initiative on issues he has designated as priorities; moreover, he has stated his conviction that episcopal conferences should have doctrinal authority, a position not encouraged in the last three decades. Second, in his encyclical, "Laudato Si" he quotes extensively throughout the letter from local episcopal conferences. This method of engagement does not diminish his role but enhances the authority of the magisterial leadership he provides the Church.

Fourth, beyond episcopal collaboration Pope Francis has found innovative ways to engage expert lay collaboration in his ministry. The forms of this are multiple, from inviting mayors of major cities around the world to discuss the environment, to engaging multinational firms to address issues of the finances of the Vatican. Here too, he reflects John Paul II's engagement with skilled professionals.

A fifth characteristic of engagement takes us from matters of style to his substantive address to issues. The Pope's address to the major issues designated above is often in a discourse of the prophetic style. He often uses sweeping characterizations (the globalization of indifference; the magic of the market; an economy of exclusion); in doing so he is not alone; each of these designations can be found in secular literature and analysis but in less powerfully symbolic statements, There is no indication that the language is purposefully meant to shock; it is rather meant to demonstrate how deeply some solutions must be rooted to be effective. Two different commutators on Pope Francis's teaching style have made similar observations. In her "Introduction" to one of the secular publications of "Laudato Si" Professor Naomi Oreskes, Professor of the History of Science at Harvard University, focuses positively on the underlying themes of the encyclical, not only the facts of the environmental crisis, but mentalities which undergird it, which she identifies as "the myths of modernity, the myth of progress and the technocratic paradigm". The words are not hers but Pope Francis's, but she finds them powerful indicators of the depth of the problem climate change holds for the world. A similar assessment of the Pope's way of addressing problems which others identify but not with the same capacity to generate responses is made by Bishop Robert McElroy of San Diego, CA.

Specifically, the pope's writings on inequality and economic justice point to the fallacies inherent in a series of major cultural assumptions that are embedded in American society. These assumptions touch upon the meaning and significance of economic inequality itself, the moral standing of free markets and the relationship between economic activity and membership in society.

To provide an adequate report of how Pope Francis's address to major issues has been received, others have found some of his comments not compelling but mistaken or in need of qualification. George Will, the dean of conservative political columnists in the United States, wrote a strong critique of both the Pope's description of problems and his proposed solutions just before the papal visit to the United States. Will described some of the Pope's positions as demonstrably false and potentially harmful to the poor.

Such comments – of strong support and equally strong critique – raise a further question about Pope Francis's engagement with major socio-economic and/or political issues like, poverty or immigration. There is no question, from my reading about his papacy, that support for the Pope's style and substance outweigh his critics inside and outside the church. A typical example is the comment of The Guardian (London) about "Laudato Si:" "The most astonishing and perhaps the most ambitious papal document of the past 100 years." On many issues Pope Francis and Pope John Paul II have spoken from similar positions. But the prophetic style of Pope Francis has galvanized support in a unique way. At the same time, and because the Holy Father is so firmly committed to issues of transcendent importance to the world and the poor of the world, one proposal could be considered. On the question of how the market economy functions and on its extension through globalization, the major difference of style of engagement between Frances and John Paul II is the way the latter moves his critique into a kind of casuistry, weighing multiple factors, balancing assessments of both the market and globalization in detached fashion. In brief, prophetic discourse and casuistic analysis can be complementary and bring different sources of strength to magisterial teaching. Both popes have stressed in encyclicals that they intended their teaching to be in continuity with their predecessors. A complementary model of these two globalist popes may be a useful contribution to engagement. This proposal seeks to maximize two styles of engagement which differ in style but not substance. The proposal may also be too absolute; certainly "Laudato Si" had casuistic dimensions to it. So, unlike assessments of the completed papacies of Leo XIII or John Paul II, evaluating the engagement of Pope Francis means analyzing a process not a finished product. The process has produced dramatic engagement for the Church and world: its final product will shape them both long after this papacy has been completed.

Engagement of "the world situation" is a permanent dimension of papal ministry. The examples examined here, along with the Second Vatican Council, are meant to provide a spectrum of styles so that future engagement can be adequately examined and supported.

11

American Attitudes on Religion in the Public Schools

Pew Research Center

The Pew Research Center is a nonpartisan fact tank that informs the public about the issues, attitudes, and trends shaping the world. Their researchers conduct public opinion polling, demographic research, content analysis, and other data-driven social science research.

The Pew Research Center examines the enduring controversy around the boundaries of religious discussion and teaching in US public schools. The report examines polling data collected by the center to show that Americans are deeply divided on the issue of whether religious sentiments should be allowed in schools, though the data suggests that most Americans believe there is room for religion in the classroom experience.

Nearly a half-century after the Supreme Court issued its landmark ruling striking down school-sponsored prayer, Americans continue to fight over the place of religion in public schools. Indeed, the classroom has become one of the most important battlegrounds in the broader conflict over religion's role in public life.

Some Americans are troubled by what they see as an effort on the part of federal courts and civil liberties advocates to exclude God and religious sentiment from public schools. Such an effort,

"Religion in the Public Schools," Pew Research Center, May 9, 2007. Reprinted by permission.

these Americans believe, infringes upon the First Amendment right to the free exercise of religion.

Civil libertarians and others, meanwhile, voice concern that conservative Christians are trying to impose their values on students of all religious stripes. Federal courts, the civil libertarians point out, have consistently interpreted the First Amendment's prohibition on the establishment of religion to forbid state sponsorship of prayer and most other religious activities in public schools.

Despite that long series of court decisions, polls show that large numbers of Americans favor looser, not tighter, limits on religion in public schools. According to an August 2006 survey by the Pew Research Center, more than two-thirds of Americans (69%) agree with the notion that "liberals have gone too far in trying to keep religion out of the schools and the government." And a clear majority (58%) favor teaching biblical creationism along with evolution in public schools.

Conflicts over religion in school are hardly new. In the 19th century, Protestants and Catholics frequently fought over Bible reading and prayer in public schools. The disputes then were over which Bible and which prayers were appropriate to use in the classroom. Some Catholics were troubled that the schools' reading materials included the King James version of the Bible, which was favored by Protestants. In 1844, fighting broke out between Protestants and Catholics in Philadelphia; a number of people died in the violence and several Catholic churches were burned. Similar conflicts erupted during the 1850s in Boston and other parts of New England. In the early 20th century, liberal Protestants and their secular allies battled religious conservatives over whether students in biology classes should be taught Charles Darwin's theory of evolution.

The Supreme Court stepped into those controversies when it determined, in *Cantwell v. Connecticut* (1940) and *Everson v. Board of Education of Ewing Township* (1947), that the First Amendment's

Free Exercise Clause and Establishment Clause applied to the states. The two clauses say, "Congress shall make no law respecting an establishment of religion, or prohibiting the free exercise thereof." Before those two court decisions, courts had applied the religion clauses only to actions of the federal government.

Soon after the *Everson* decision, the Supreme Court began specifically applying the religion clauses to activities in public schools. In its first such case, *McCollum v. Board of Education* (1948), the high court invalidated the practice of having religious instructors from different denominations enter public schools to offer religious lessons during the school day to students whose parents requested them. A key factor in the court's decision was that the lessons took place in the schools. Four years later, in *Zorach v. Clauson*, the court upheld an arrangement by which public schools excused students during the school day so they could attend religious classes away from school property.

Beginning in the 1960s, the court handed religious conservatives a series of major defeats. It began with the landmark 1962 ruling, in *Engel v. Vitale*, that school-sponsored prayer, even if it were nonsectarian, violated the Establishment Clause. Since then, the Supreme Court has pushed forward, from banning organized Bible reading for religious and moral instruction in 1963 to prohibiting prayers at high school football games 2000.

In these and other decisions, the court has repeatedly stressed that the Constitution prohibits public schools from indoctrinating children in religion. But it is not always easy to determine exactly what constitutes indoctrination or school sponsorship of religious activities. For example, can a class on the Bible as literature be taught without a bias for or against the idea that the Bible is religious truth? Can students be compelled to participate in a Christmas-themed music program? Sometimes students themselves, rather than teachers, administrators or coaches, bring their faith into school activities. For instance, when a student invokes gratitude to God in a valedictory address, or a high school football player offers a prayer in a huddle, is the school legally responsible for their religious expression?

The issues are complicated by other constitutional guarantees. For instance, the First Amendment also protects freedom of speech and freedom of association. Religious groups have cited those guarantees in support of student religious speech and in efforts to obtain school sponsorship and resources for student religious clubs.

The right of a student or student club to engage in religious speech or activities on school property may, however, conflict with other protections, such as the right of students to avoid harassment. In one recent case, for example, a federal appeals court approved a high school's decision to prohibit a student from wearing a T-shirt containing a biblical passage condemning homosexuality. Because the student had graduated by the time the Supreme Court granted his appeal, the Supreme Court ordered the lower court to vacate its ruling and dismiss the case.

In another instance of conflicting rights, some student religious groups want the right to exclude students who do not share the groups' beliefs, specifically on questions of sexuality. For example, the Christian Legal Society, which has chapters in many law schools, is embroiled in litigation over its policy that only students who believe that sex outside of heterosexual marriage is a sin can serve in leadership positions.

As these more recent conflicts show, public schools remain a battlefield where the religious interests of parents, students, administrators and teachers often clash. The conflicts affect classroom curricula, high school football games, student clubs, graduation ceremonies — and the lives of everyone with an interest in public education.

12

President Bush's Faith-Based Initiative
Joseph Loconte

Joseph Loconte, PhD, is an associate professor of history at the King's College in New York City. He previously served as a distinguished visiting professor at the School of Public Policy at Pepperdine University, and was a senior fellow at the Ethics and Public Policy Center in Washington, DC.

Joseph Loconte examines the controversy surrounding former President George W. Bush's plan to provide federal support to certain religious organizations involved in social welfare work, known as the faith-based initiative. Loconte expresses his support for Bush's initiative, asserting that the government should not shun private religious groups, insisting that they are among the most effective organizations at addressing social issues and consequently should be granted more federal help. He also hopes that the government will start to dispel the notion that federal funding leads to increased government meddling in private organizations.

President Bush's plan to promote and finance religious charities has been attacked by liberals as a ploy for government-funded religion, and by conservatives as a Trojan horse for government control over religion. Both scenarios are dubious, and both ignore the real import of the president's agenda. The Bush plan would open up new sources of federal dollars to faith-based providers to

"President Bush's Faith-Based Initiative," by Joseph Loconte, The Heritage Foundation, July 18, 2001. Reprinted by permission.

run programs ranging from juvenile delinquency to job training. That could help inner-city ministries shunned by government or overlooked by private donors. For children at risk of slipping into poverty or violence, that's a good step.

But making federal grants available to religious charities is the least important part of the president's initiative. Many private organizations believe that government's helping hand will become a wagging finger. They won't get involved with public money, no matter what the rules are. And even if they do, federal help would amount to just a fraction of the $74 billion that one study estimates is donated each year to churches and religious charities.

What's at stake is something much larger: the false assumption that religious belief carries no advantage over unbelief in tackling social problems. Bush is using public policy and his bully pulpit to send a message, 'Government must not discriminate against groups that are guided by their belief in God as they help their neighbors. They are community paramedics, not civic pariahs.'

Already that message is resonating. Officials at corrections departments in Michigan, New Mexico and Nebraska, mindful of the president's support of faith-based rehabilitation programs, have called Prison Fellowship to work with inmates and ex-offenders. In Sacramento, African-American and Latino churches are saying no to public money, yet mobilizing volunteers to work with families on welfare. The city has sent them over 200 clients for help in job searches and preparation. In Philadelphia, Mayor John Street has set up an office to negotiate church-state agreements and appealed to congregations to adopt failing city schools. In less than six months, they have recruited over 500 volunteers to mentor at-risk kids. Hundreds of congregations are involved in similar efforts in Los Angeles, Chicago and Boston. These agreements would have been unthinkable a few years ago. They are becoming routine. The failure of secular bureaucratic programs to help people effectively is part of the reason. But surely a faith-friendly White House is changing the way many people think about the importance of religion in public life.

America has a history of poverty fighters whose faith sustained profound acts of sacrifice on behalf of the most vulnerable among us. As Bush put it recently in Philadelphia, America's founding documents give us religious liberty in principle. These Americans show us religious liberty in action. We need more of this variety of religious freedom, not less.

13

It's Time to Separate Church and State Marriages

Bryan Cones

Bryan Cones is associate editor of U.S. Catholic *magazine in Chicago, Illinois. He holds a master's degree in theology from Catholic Theological Union in Chicago and was formed in the habits of liturgical prayer by the Benedictine monks of Conception Abbey in Conception, Missouri.*

Bryan Cones examines polling data collected by U.S. Catholic *magazine on Catholic attitudes toward same-sex marriage. He argues that the broad diversity of opinion, both within the Catholic community and in American society in general, indicates that religious and state-sponsored marriage agreements should be separate. He asserts that this would enable priests and their congregation to avoid the risk of violating their religious beliefs while also allowing the civil rights of the LGBT community to be respected.*

The June 2013 Supreme Court rulings that struck down portions of the federal Defense of Marriage Act and overturned California's Proposition 8 marked a major turning point in the debate over whether same-sex couples should have access to the civil institution of marriage. That debate, which began slowly with a Massachusetts State Supreme Court ruling; similar rulings in Iowa, California, and Vermont; and successive state legislatures'

"It's Time to Separate Church and State Marriages," by Bryan Cones, U.S. Catholic, February 2014. Reprinted by permission.

legal recognition of same-sex marriage or parallel civil union, is fast heading toward a conclusion.

The Internal Revenue Service's August decision to grant married filing status to married same-sex couples even if they live in a state that does not recognize their union is further indication that, on the national level, the question of whether same-sex couples can marry has largely been determined.

These developments, however, continue to expose wide divides in society about the definition and meaning of marriage, no less in the Catholic Church. The Catholic bishops of this country have been nearly univocal in denouncing any attempt to redefine civil marriage. Individual bishops have devoted large amounts of financial and other diocesan resources in political activity to oppose changes to the civil law.

Rank-and-file Catholics, meanwhile, seem to be leaning the other way on the issue. Poll after poll shows Catholics favoring legal recognition of same-sex couples—either in marriage or civil unions—by large margins. A Public Religion Research Institute poll in March 2011 found that 43 percent of Catholic respondents support full civil marriage rights, with another 31 percent in favor of civil unions; a poll two years later found that 54 percent support full civil marriage rights with 38 percent opposed, a complete reversal of the findings as recently as 2008.

Given the shift in marriage's civil legal definition to include same-sex couples, it is time that Catholic conversations about the issue recognize that we are talking about two different realities when we use the word "marriage"—a legal contract on the civil side, and a sacramental covenant between two baptized people on the other—and adjust our practice accordingly. Doing so would allow Catholics to have a fruitful intramural conversation about our theological understanding of the sacrament of marriage without being entangled in the question of whether families and couples who don't fit that vision should have access to the legal benefits and duties that go with its civil parallel. It would also acknowledge what should be obvious to everyone: Even if civil and religious marriage were once a single entity, the ties uniting those two dimensions have now almost completely unraveled.

One doesn't have to look far into Christian history to find differences between a general societal view of marriage and what became the Christian vision. Jesus' condemnation of divorce (Mark 10:2-12; Matt. 19:3-9) questioned the practices of some rabbis in his own Jewish community who permitted marriages to be easily dissolved. Paul's insistence that women had rights within marriage, to sex for example (1 Cor. 7:1-10), were revolutionary in a Greco-Roman culture in which women were treated as property and divorce was common for the sake of cementing family alliances. His repetition of Jesus' teaching against divorce (with some exception) made clear that marriage was practiced differently in the household of God than in civil society.

Despite the New Testament witnesses, ancient Christian practice around marriage does not become clear until about the fourth century, as the settlement joining the church to the Roman Empire was becoming firm. Once bishops and priests became civil authorities, the civil and religious dimensions of marriage also became joined—a situation that endured until the modern period.

Many liberal democracies in Europe and Latin America have long required a civil marriage first, followed by a separate religious ceremony, or convalidation, if the couple so desires. But the effects of the "marriage" between church and state in this country are evident every time a priest signs a civil marriage license, the only time a religious leader still acts as a civil servant in the United States—a practice that is against the law in countries such as Mexico.

Indeed, the fear of many Catholics who oppose same-sex marriage is that priests, since they act as civil authorities in performing marriage ceremonies, will be "forced" to solemnize the marriage of same-sex couples, thus contravening the church's teaching. The easiest way to solve that problem is for priests to stop signing any civil marriage licenses—a duty that can surely be left to a local judge—and only officiating sacramental weddings. Forcing couples to essentially be "married" twice may have the unfortunate side effect of some couples skipping the religious marriage altogether, but even that may open up an opportunity for Catholics to tease out the difference between a civil and a sacramental marriage.

Beyond the relationship between church and state on the matter of marriage, however, there's simply no denying that marriage in any form isn't the institution it used to be. Sociologists and historians, notably Stephanie Coontz, have documented the shift from models of marriage focused on economic productivity and procreation to our contemporary "companionate model," with focus on the relationship and well-being of the partners. That shift has no doubt fuelled society's acceptance of civil partnerships between persons of the same sex.

While many defenders of "traditional" marriage may insist that marriage is and has always been by definition between a man and a woman, that now holds true only when talking about the sacrament. When it comes to civil marriage, both state legislatures and the courts have already changed the legal definition, just as they did in the matter of no-fault divorce laws, thus undermining the "lifelong" portion of the marital definition. History makes clear that, at least when it comes to civil marriage, the definition has been a moving target.

Catholic teaching in the past 100 years has itself undergone a similar shift. While Pius XI's 1930 encyclical *Casti Connubii* continued to characterize marriage primarily as a contract with little specifically theological significance, Vatican II's 1965 pastoral constitution *Gaudium et Spes* and Pope Paul VI's 1968 encyclical *Humanae Vitae* shifted to the biblical language of marriage as a "covenant" between the spouses. Pope John Paul II's "theology of the body" elevated church language about the good of marriage, and sex within it, to a further dignity that would likely make Pius XI blush.

The so-called "unitive principle" of marriage that appears in contemporary Catholic teaching—what *Gaudium et Spes* calls the "mutual help and service to each other through an intimate union of their persons and of their actions"—reflects the broader societal shift toward the companionate model of marriage. Where Catholic teaching goes beyond this model is in its emphasis on procreation as a critical dimension of marriage. While a strictly civil marriage need not include both dimensions—any more than it must include a lifelong commitment—they cannot be absent from the sacramental union of two baptized persons (at least when both partners are physically capable of having children).

Separating religious marriage from its civil counterpart will of course not overcome every social, political, and theological challenge related to same-sex relationships. Lesbian and gay Catholics will likely continue to make known their views on marriage and to ask Catholics to reconsider the church's teaching on the matter, as is their right under the Code of Canon Law as baptized people (canon 212).

We may, however, hope for some new beginnings. Catholics who wish to can celebrate with gay and lesbian neighbors, friends, and family members the new and important steps our society has taken toward granting civil rights to same-sex couples with less need to explain how one can be "a good Catholic" and still support the civil rights of those couples. People concerned with the religious definition of marriage will be free to pursue its theological dimensions, and all sides will hopefully benefit from a more charitable debate on the matter.

Priests, freed from their civil obligations, will have no concern over being required to violate their beliefs. And bishops, relieved of the need to bankroll ever more expensive political initiatives, can devote time and resources to strengthening the sacramental dimensions of Catholic marriage and family life.

Perhaps together we will come up with a creative new beginning to Catholic reflection on human sexuality and marriage, one that still critiques and challenges the world around us, as the gospel always does, while also offering the encouragement and hope that is the hallmark of the Good News.

And the Survey Says...

1. I Believe that Same Sex Couples Should:
33% - Be able to enter into a sacramental marriage in the Catholic Church.
20% - Be able to have a religious marriage in churches/denominations that choose to recognize such unions, but never be married in the Catholic Church.
17% - Be able to enter into civil unions, but marriages should be reserved to "one man and one woman."
10% - Be able to enter into a civil marriage but not a religious marriage.
7% - Not have their relationship officially recognized by the state or the church.
13% - Other

2. I Believe that Civil and Religious Marriages Ought to Be Separated:
84% - Agree
11% - Disagree
5% - Other

3. If Couples Were Required to Have Both a Civil Wedding and a Separate Sacramental Wedding, Fewer Catholic Couples Would Get Married in the Church
37% - Agree
50% - Disagree
13% - Other
Representative of "other":
"Depends on who counts as a 'Catholic couple.' Those who are serious about the faith would choose both."

4. I Have Friends or Family Who Have Entered Into:
30% - A same-sex civil marriage.
19% - A same-sex civil union.
13% - A same-sex religious marriage.

15% - None of the above, because the same-sex couples I know do not live in a state nor belong to a church that recognizes their partnership.

23% - I do not know anyone in a same-sex relationship.

5. A Marriage Can Only Take Place in the Church and Therefore the State Should Be the One to Stop Performing "Marriages" for Any and All Couples

7% - Agree
87% - Disagree
6% - Other

6. Even If Priests Stop Performing Civil Marriage Ceremonies, the Church Still Needs to Campaign Against the Acceptance of Same-Sex Civil Marriages

13% - Agree
78% - Disagree
9% - Other
Representative of "other":
"Campaign, no. Explain, yes."

7. The Definition of Marriage as "One Man and One Woman" Should Be True for Both Religious and Civil Partnerships

16% - Agree
76% - Disagree
8% - Other

Results are based on survey responses from 435 USCatholic.org visitors.

14

The Christian Right and the New Right

USHistory.org

USHistory.org is a website operated and owned by the Independence Hall Association of Philadelphia. The association is a nonprofit organization that was founded in 1942. The website offers thousands of pages of US history in keeping with the association's mission to educate the public about American history.

This viewpoint discusses the rise of the New Right—of which the Christian Right is part—at the end of the 1970s in the United States. It explains how this political movement arose from the social changes and culture wars of the 1960s and 1970s, including the Roe v. Wade *decision, which outraged many in the religious community and other conservatives. The various Christian communities that made up the Christian Right are also discussed.*

Not everyone was happy with the social changes brought forth in America in the 1960s and 1970s. When *Roe v. Wade* guaranteed the right to an abortion, a fervent pro-life movement dedicated to protecting the "unborn child" took root.

Antifeminists rallied against the Equal Rights Amendment and the eroding traditional family unit. Many ordinary Americans were shocked by the sexual permissiveness found in films and magazines. Those who believed homosexuality was sinful lambasted the newly

---

"The New Right," USHistory.org, http://www.ushistory.org/us/58e.asp. Licensed under CC BY 4.0 International.

vocal gay rights movement. As the divorce and crime rates rose, an increasing number of Americans began to blame the liberal welfare establishment for social maladies. A cultural war unfolded at the end of the 1970s.

Enter the New Right

The New Right was a combination of Christian religious leaders, conservative business bigwigs who claimed that environmental and labor regulations were undermining the competitiveness of American firms in the global market, and fringe political groups.

There was nothing new about political and economic conservatism. Barry Goldwater based his 1964 Presidential campaign on the premise that the New Deal should be reversed. He declared that big government was the greatest threat to American liberty. Social spending and welfare needed to be cut to reduce the tax burden on individuals and families. Government regulations were inhibiting economic growth and personal freedoms. When foreign competition made inroads against American corporations in the 1970s, many people began to believe Goldwater had been right. Big business wielded its financial resources as a backbone of the New Right movement.

Another linchpin of the conservative backlash was the Christian Right. Since the 1950s, members of the evangelical Christian denominations increased fivefold. By the mid-1970s, over a quarter of adult Americans identified themselves as born-again Christians.

The Christian Right had many faces. Fundamentalists such as Jerry Falwell believed in a literal interpretation of the Bible. Pentacostalists such as Pat Robertson claimed the Holy Spirit communicated directly with people on a regular basis.

Despite theological divisions, all evangelical leaders agreed that America was experiencing a moral decline. They explained that homosexuality was a crime against God, and that a woman's place was in the home in support of her family. They criticized the "liberal" media for corrupting America's youth. They chided the courts for taking religion out of the public schools and supported private Christian academies and homeschooling as alternatives.

Many Catholic Americans agreed with the sentiments of the New Right. The reforming spirit of the Catholic Church reached its high water mark in the 1960s with a convention called Vatican II. Latin was dropped as a requirement for the mass. Lay people were given a greater role in Church services. Support was given for ecumenical outreach to other Christian denominations and Jewish synagogues.

Social politics of the time forged connections between Catholic and Protestant leaders. Abortion and "family rights" were seen as areas of common ground. The appointment of the conservative John Paul II in 1979 marked an end to the reform spirit within the Church.

New Right leaders were highly organized and understood the potential of mass telecommunications. Pat Robertson formed the Christian Broadcasting Network to send his message. The PTL (Praise the Lord) Club led by Jim Bakker transmitted faith healing and raucous religious revival to the largest viewing audience of any daily program in the world. They built massive databases containing the names and addresses of potential financial contributors and regularly solicited funds. In 1979, Jerry Falwell formed the Moral Majority, Inc. This group and hundreds of others raised money to defeat liberal senators, representatives, and governors. They sought to control school boards on the local level to advance their conservative agenda. Ronald Reagan freely accepted contributions from the New Right on his way to the Presidency in 1980.

Like most movements, the New Right contained an extremist element. Racial hatred groups like the Ku Klux Klan and the American Nazi Party joined the outcry against American moral decline. Ultra-libertarian militia groups formed in many states dedicated to attacking the American government they believed had become far too invasive. They steadfastly supported the right to bear arms as a means to defend themselves from tyranny. Some groups began stockpiling arsenals. These organizations interpreted the term "cultural war" in the most literal, ominous sense.

For many, the end of the '70s seemed shrouded in a dark malaise.

But morning in America was about to dawn.

Organizations to Contact

The editors have compiled the following list of organizations concerned with the issues debated in this book. The descriptions are derived from materials provided by the organizations. All have publications or information available for interested readers. The list was compiled on the date of publication of the present volume; the information provided here may change. Be aware that many organizations take several weeks or longer to respond to inquiries, so allow as much time as possible.

Advocates for Faith and Freedom
24910 Las Brisas Road, Suite 109
Murrieta, CA 92562
phone: (951) 600-4996
email: info@faith-freedom.com
website: www.faith-freedom.com

Advocates for Faith and Freedom is a nonprofit law firm dedicated to protecting religious liberty in the courts. Their mission is to engage in cases that will uphold religious liberty and America's heritage and to educate Americans about their fundamental constitutional rights.

American Center for Law and Justice (ACLJ)
PO Box 90555
Washington, DC 20090-0555
phone: (800) 342-2255
website: www.aclj.org

The American Center for Law and Justice is a tax-exempt, not-for-profit, religious corporation specifically dedicated to the ideal that religious freedom and freedom of speech are inalienable, God-given rights. The Center's purpose is to engage legal, legislative, and cultural issues by implementing an effective strategy of advocacy, education, and litigation to ensure that those rights are protected under the law.

Americans for Religious Liberty
PO Box 6656
Silver Spring, MD 20916
phone: (301) 460-1111
email: arlinc@verizon.net
website: www.arlinc.org

The mission of Americans for Religious Liberty is to defend the core constitutional principle of separation of church and state and, in so doing, help to preserve the nation's historic tradition of religious, intellectual, and moral freedom in a secular state. Providing a public voice for those who support these aims, and in cooperation with like-minded organizations and individuals, Americans for Religious Liberty pursues its mission through research, education, advocacy, and publishing.

Bill of Rights Institute
1310 North Courthouse Rd. #620
Arlington, VA 22201
phone: (703) 894-1776
email: info@billofrightsinstitute.org
website: http://www.billofrightsinstitute.org/

Established in September 1999, the Bill of Rights Institute is a 501(c)(3) nonprofit educational organization that works to engage, educate, and empower individuals with a passion for the freedom and opportunity that exist in a free society. The Institute develops educational resources and programs for a network of more than 50,000 educators and 70,000 students nationwide.

First Amendment Center at Vanderbilt University
John Seigenthaler Center
1207 18th Ave. S.
Nashville, TN 37212
phone: (615) 727-1600
website: www.firstamendmentcenter.org

The First Amendment Center supports the First Amendment and builds understanding of its core freedoms through education, information, and entertainment. The center serves as a forum for the study and exploration of free-expression issues, including freedom of speech, of the press, and of religion, and the rights to assemble and to petition the government. Founded by John Seigenthaler, the First Amendment Center is an operating program of the Freedom Forum and is associated with the Newseum and the Diversity Institute.

Foundation for Individual Rights in Education (FIRE)
510 Walnut St., Suite 1250
Philadelphia, PA 19106
phone: (215) 717-FIRE
email: fire@thefire.org
website: www.thefire.org

The mission of FIRE is to defend and sustain individual rights at America's colleges and universities. These rights include freedom of speech, legal equality, due process, religious liberty, and sanctity of conscience—the essential qualities of individual liberty and dignity. FIRE's core mission is to protect the unprotected and to educate the public and communities of concerned Americans about the threats to these rights on our campuses and about the means to preserve them.

Interfaith Youth Core (IFYC)
141 W. Jackson Blvd, Suite 3200
Chicago, IL 60604
phone: (312) 573-8825
email: info@ifyc.org
website: www.ifyc.org

IFYC is a national nonprofit organization working towards an America where people of different faiths, worldviews, and traditions can bridge differences and find common values to build a shared life together. IFYC partners with American colleges and universities and works to equip students, educators, and whole institutions with the vision, knowledge, and skills to advance ideals of tolerance, diversity, and religious freedom on campus and far beyond.

National Constitution Center
Independence Mall
525 Arch Street
Philadelphia, PA 19106
phone: (215) 409-6600
website: www.constitutioncenter.org

The National Constitution Center is the first and only institution in America established by Congress to "disseminate information about the United States Constitution on a nonpartisan basis in order to increase the awareness and understanding of the Constitution among the American people." The Constitution Center brings the United States Constitution to life by hosting interactive exhibits and constitutional conversations and inspires active citizenship by celebrating the American constitutional tradition.

Southern Poverty Law Center
400 Washington Avenue
Montgomery, AL 36104
phone: (334) 956-8200
website: www.splcenter.org

The Southern Poverty Law Center monitors hate groups and other extremists throughout the United States and exposes their activities to law enforcement agencies, the media, and the public.

Bibliography

Books

Damon T. Berry. *Blood & Faith: Christianity in American White Nationalism.* Syracuse, NY: Syracuse University Press, 2017.

Matthew Bowman. *Christian: The Politics of a Word in America.* Cambridge, MA: Harvard University Press, 2018.

Forrest Church. *The Separation of Church and State: Writings on a Fundamental Freedom by America's Founders.* Boston, MA: Beacon Press, 2004.

Ryan L. Claassen. *Godless Democrats and Pious Republicans: Party Activists, Party Capture, and the 'God Gap'.* New York, NY: Cambridge University Press, 2015.

John Fea. *Believe Me: The Evangelical Road to Donald Trump.* Grand Rapids, MI: Eerdmans Publishing Company, 2018.

Frances Fitzgerald. *The Evangelicals: The Struggle to Shape America.* New York, NY: Simon and Schuster, 2017.

Greg Forster. *The Contested Public Square: The Crisis of Christianity and Politics.* Downer's Grove, IL: InterVarsity Press, 2008.

Michael Gerson and Peter Wehner. *City of Man: Religion and Politics in a New Era.* Chicago, IL: Moody Publishers, 2010.

R. Marie Griffith. *Moral Combat: How Sex Divided American Christians and Fractured American Politics.* New York, NY: Basic Books, 2017.

Jonathan Haidt. *The Righteous Mind: Why Good People Are Divided by Politics and Religion.* New York, NY: Random House, 2012.

Kevin M. Kruse. *One Nation Under God: How Corporate America Invented Christian America.* New York, NY: Basic Books, 2015.

Jonathan Leeman. *How the Nations Rage: Rethinking Faith and Politics in a Divided Age.* Nashville, TN: Nelson Books, 2018.

Andrew R. Lewis. *The Rights Turn in Conservative Christian Politics: How Abortion Transformed the Culture Wars.* New York, NY: Cambridge University Press, 2017.

Michele F. Margolis. *From Politics to the Pews: How Partisanship and the Political Environment Shape Religious Identity.* Chicago, IL: University of Chicago Press, 2018.

Jon Meacham. *American Gospel: God, the Founding Fathers, and the Making of a Nation.* New York, NY: Random House, 2006.

Martha Nussbaum. *Liberty of Conscience: In Defense of America's Tradition of Religious Equality.* New York, NY: Basic Books, 2008.

Tisa Wenger. *Religious Freedom: The Contested History of an American Ideal.* Chapel Hill, NC: University of North Carolina Press, 2017.

Daniel K. Williams. *God's Own Party: The Making of the Christian Right.* New York, NY: Oxford University Press, 2010.

Periodicals and Internet Sources

Perry Bacon Jr. and Dhrumil Mehta, "Religious Democrats, Young Republicans: What the Stereotypes Miss About Both Parties," *FiveThirtyEight*, March 23, 2018, https://fivethirtyeight.com/features/religious-democrats-young-republicans-what-the-stereotypes-miss-about-both-parties/

Randall Balmer, "Under Trump, America's Religious Right Is Rewriting its Code of Ethics," *Guardian,* February 18, 2018, https://www.theguardian.com/commentisfree/2018/feb/18/donald-trump-evangelicals-code-of-ethics

Nigel Barber, "Why Religion Rules American Politics," *Huffington Post*, September 19, 2012, https://www.huffingtonpost.com/nigel-barber/why-religion-rules-americ_b_1690433.html

Julie Butters, "Why American Can't Separate Religion and Politics and What That Means for the 2016 Elections," Boston University College of Arts and Sciences, Fall 2015, http://www.bu.edu/cas/magazine/fall15/america/

John D. Carlson, "Losing Our Civil Religion," *Religion & Politics*, September 26, 2017, http://religionandpolitics.org/2017/09/26/losing-our-civil-religion/chr

Alexandra DeSanctis, "Why Progressivism and Religion Don't Go Together," *National Review*, July 7, 2017, https://www.nationalreview.com/2017/07/democrats-religion-problem-progressivism-faith-inherently-contradictory/

Garrett Epps, "The Constitution Doesn't Separate Church and State," *Atlantic*, June 15, 2011, https://www.theatlantic.com/national/archive/2011/06/constitutional-myth-4-the-constitution-doesnt-separate-church-and-state/240481/

Bill Flax, "The True Meaning of Separation of Church and State," *Forbes*, July 9, 2011, https://www.forbes.com/sites/billflax/2011/07/09/the-true-meaning-of-separation-of-church-and-state/#2265b4675d02

Dale Hansen, "Yes There Is a Constitutional Separation of Church and State," *Huffington Post*, September 21, 2016, https://www.huffingtonpost.com/dale-hansen/yes-there-is-a-constituti_b_8171550.html

Bibliography

Benjamin E. Park, "The Revolutionary Roots of America's Religious Nationalism," *Religion & Politics*, March 20, 2018, http://religionandpolitics.org/2018/03/20/the-revolutionary-roots-of-americas-religious-nationalism/

Bre Payton, "The Religion of the Democratic Party Is Abortion and Brunch," *Federalist*, February 15, 2018, http://thefederalist.com/2018/02/15/religion-democratic-party-abortion-brunch/

Charles P. Pierce, "Roy Moore Is Exactly What the Republican Party Is All About," *Esquire*, November 10, 2017, https://www.esquire.com/news-politics/politics/a13518962/roy-moore-is-who-republicans-are/

Steven Shepard, "Study: Political Parties Transformed by Racial and Religious Changes," *Politico*, September 6, 2017, https://www.politico.com/story/2017/09/06/political-parties-religion-race-242322

Graham Vyse, "Trump and the Republicans Are Redefining 'Religious Freedom' to Favor Christians," *New Republic*, February 16, 2017, https://newrepublic.com/article/140645/trump-republicans-redefining-religious-freedom-favor-christians

Michael Wear, "Why Democrats Must Regain the Trust of Religious Voters," *Atlantic*, November 21, 2017, https://www.theatlantic.com/politics/archive/2017/11/why-democrats-must-regain-faith-among-religious-voters/546434/

Daniel K. Williams, "The Democrats' Religion Problem," *New York Times*, June 23, 2017, https://www.nytimes.com/2017/06/23/opinion/democrats-religion-jon-ossoff.html

Index

A

abolition movement, 8, 36
abortion, 9, 110, 114, 116
Americans for Tax Reform, 45
Association of Christian Schools International et al. v. Roman Stearns et al., 81
atheists, 15, 47–50, 86
Audi, Robert, 21–24

B

Baptist faith, 7, 11, 26–27, 37, 51–64, 65–68
Beecher, Catherine, 32–33
Benedict XVI, Pope, 44, 46, 94
Bible, 13, 14, 19, 53, 71, 72, 76–79, 101–102, 115
Black Lives Matter, 39
Bryan, William Jennings, 71–74
Buddhism, 29
Buffet, Warren, 43–44
Bush, George W., 45, 104–106
Bussey, Barry, 7

C

Cain, Herman, 44
Calvinism, 17, 20
Cantwell v. Connecticut, 101–102
Catholicism, 15, 16, 41–46, 82–99
Christian fundamentalists, 15, 20, 22, 115
Christian Right, the, 114–117
civil rights, 8, 26–35, 36, 59, 62, 87, 111
Civil War, 37, 70
Cold War, 84, 92–94
Cones, Bryan, 107–113
Creationism, 16, 75–76
Curtotti, Michael, 26–35

D

Darrow, Clarence, 72–74
Darwin, Charles, 69, 70–81, 101
death penalty, 9, 53
Defense of Marriage Act, 107

E

Ecklund, Elaine Howard, 47–50
Edwards v. Aguillard, 76–77, 78
Egan, Anthony, 8, 15–25
Engel v. Vitale, 102
Epperson v. Arkansas, 74–76, 78
eugenics, 71–72
Evangelical movement, 9
Evans, Christopher H., 36–40
Everson v. Board of Education, 74–76, 101–102
evolution debate, 69–81, 101

F

faith-based initiative, 104–106
First Amendment, 67, 68, 74, 75, 101–103

Index

Francis, Pope, 41, 83, 94–99
Freiler v. Tangipahoa Parish (La.) Board of Education, 78

G

Gandhi, Mohandas, 33–34
Gates, Bill, 43–44
Gehring, John, 41–46
Gilroy, Paul, 31–33
Gingrich, Newt, 42, 44
Goldwater, Barry, 115
Gorbachev, Michael, 92
Grimké, Angelina, 32–33

H

Harris, Sam, 9
heresy, 17, 19
Hitchens, Christopher, 9
Hittinger, Russell, 88–89
human rights, 20, 30–31

I

"In God We Trust," 14
intelligent design, 79–81

J

James, Suzanne, 64
Jefferson, Thomas, 7, 11
Jesuit, 15, 43, 95, 96
Jesuit Institute of South Africa, 15
Jesus, 15, 37, 40, 109
John XXIII, Pope, 20, 44, 90
John Paul II, Pope, 44, 82–83, 84–94, 110, 116
Judaism, 28, 109, 116

K

Kammer, Father Fred, 43
Kennedy, D. James, 11–14
Kent, John, 18
King, Martin Luther, Jr., 25–35, 38, 40
Kitzmiller v. Dover Area School District, 80–81

L

Lemon v. Kurtzman, 76–77, 81
Leo XIII, Pope, 20, 99
Lerner, Michael, 39
LGBT equality, 39, 107–113
Liberalism, 8, 17, 19, 36, 89
Loconte, Joseph, 104–106
Lutheran faith, 20, 38

M

Marx, Karl, 8, 71
Masci, David, 69–81
McCaig, Amy, 48–50
McLean v. Arkansas Board of Education, 76
Mill, John Stuart, 8, 18
Moses, 14, 29
Murray, John Courtney, 89–92
Muste, A. J., 38, 40

N

New Right, the, 114–117
Nietzsche, Friedrich, 8
Nobel Peace Prize, 30
Norquist, Grover, 45

P

Park, Benjamin E., 9
Paul VI, Pope, 84, 110
Phelps, Fred Waldron, Sr., 51–64, 65
Pinker, Steven, 9
Pius XI, Pope, 19, 90, 110
political Islam, 16
Pontifical Academy of Social Sciences, the, 82–99
Protestantism, 70–71

R

racism, 27, 30, 38
Rahner, Karl, 93–94
Rauschenbusch, Walter, 36–40
Reagan, Ronald, 9, 116
religion in public schools, 9, 16, 100
religious extremism, 15, 16
religious left, 36–40
Rice University, 47–50
Roe v. Wade, 114
Roosevelt, Eleanor, 34

S

Sachs, Albie, 28–29
Samaritans, 17
same-sex marriage, 9, 107–113
Scalia, Antonin, 77–78
Schaerr, Gene, 67–68
science and atheism, 47–50
scientific rationalism, 19
Second Vatican Council, 82–99
secular age, the, 15–25
Selman v. Cobb County School District, 79
separation of church and state, 11–14, 16, 17, 110
slavery, 27, 32, 70, 83
social Darwinism, 71
social gospel movement, 36–40
State of Tennessee v. Scopes, 69, 72–74
Stout, Jeffrey, 16
superstition, 8, 15, 72

T

taxation, 41–46
Taylor, Charles, 18–19, 24
Tea Party, 41–46
terrorism, 16, 95
Totenberg, Nina, 65–69
Trinity Decision, 13

U

United Nations, 84, 94
Universal Declaration of Human Rights, 31–34
USHistory.org, 114–117

W

Wagnon, Joan, 52, 57, 60
Wallis, Jim, 39, 40
Wellman, James, 39–40
Westboro Baptist Church, 51–64, 65–69

Z

Zorach v. Clauson, 102

WITHDRAWN

$39.40

LONGWOOD PUBLIC LIBRARY
800 Middle Country Road
Middle Island, NY 11953
(631) 924-6400
longwoodlibrary.org

LIBRARY HOURS

Monday-Friday	9:30 a.m. - 9:00 p.m.
Saturday	9:30 a.m. - 5:00 p.m.
Sunday (Sept-June)	1:00 p.m. - 5:00 p.m.